D0443032

BITCH IS THE NEW BLACK

HELENA ANDREWS

Bitch

IS THE NEW BLACK

A Memoir

HARPER

An Imprint of HarperCollins*Publishers*

www.harpercollins.com

SANTA CLARA PUBLIC LIBRARY
2635 Homestead Road
Santa Clara, CA 95051

Many of the names in this book have been changed in order to protect certain people's privacy and prevent Facebook stalking. Gina is Gina because all her suggestions were dumb. And Frances, my mother, is Frances, my mother, because who else could she be?

BITCH IS THE NEW BLACK. Copyright © 2010 by Helena Andrews. All rights reserved. Printed in the United States of America. No part of this book may be used or reproduced in any manner whatsoever without written permission except in the case of brief quotations embodied in critical articles and reviews. For information, address HarperCollins Publishers, 10 East 53rd Street, New York, NY 10022.

HarperCollins books may be purchased for educational, business, or sales promotional use. For information, please write: Special Markets Department, HarperCollins Publishers, 10 East 53rd Street, New York, NY 10022.

FIRST EDITION

Designed by Janet M. Evans

Library of Congress Cataloging-in-Publication Data has been applied for.

ISBN: 978-0-06-177882-7

10 11 12 13 14   OV/RRD 10 9 8 7 6 5 4 3 2 1

Dear Toto, Kansas sucks. I get why you chose Oz. Advanced balloon technology is on the rise, so maybe we'll see each other again. Love, Cinderella.

Contents

BITCH IS THE NEW BLACK

DIRTY ASTRONAUT DIAPERS

Dex10 (12:01:10 p.m.): hey

Dex10 (12:01:40 p.m.): stop it!

Dex10 (12:03:10 p.m.): you win

Dex10 (12:05:00 p.m.): AHHHHHHHH

Copy, paste, and send. "Dude, what the eff does he even *mean* by this? Win what? What, in the name of bearded carpenter Jesus, have I won?"

I'm consulting the oracle Gina, as is my ritual. But instead of divining my future from a mound of discarded hot wings, Gi offers me this:

"Dude, you ain't won shit."

He's the Nigerian E-mail Scam of ex-sorta-boyfriends, trying to seduce me over cyberspace with promises of riches in the real world. Problem is, I'm black *and* I have a vagina, so my *Waiting to Exhale* intuition tells me this shit ain't for real. In the history of the world, black women have won approximately three things—freedom, a hot comb, and Robin Thicke. With a track record like that, it's obvious that the catchphrase "you win" is exactly that—a verbal fly trap meant to trick me into letting him back in, into loving him again. All Dex10 needs next is my routing number and date of birth.

Too bad my DOB wasn't yesterday. I refuse to write his ass back. I can't. And even though I've been planning our pretend wedding for the past six months, pressing my would-be ring finger on the keyboard would be even more pathetic. So I'm staring blankly at the blank space in our dialogue box. Maybe we *should* be dialoguing. Maybe he'll tell me all the things he couldn't say when I was so obviously his and so ready to hear them and so not in my PJs with my hair in a topknot. My stomach's tied up in one too. Maybe he's come around. Maybe he's chaaanged.

Maybe I'm an idiot.

If I'm not—an idiot, that is—then undergoing evasive maneuvers makes perfect sense. I'm not ready for Dex10 to boldly go where no man has gone before, flicking the switch in rooms usually kept dark. Usually I'll try it at least once with the lights on, but not this time. See, he's done all this before. He's already made me fall in love, then out, then in, then upside down, and then over it. So now, after having succeeded beyond all odds in ignoring his ass for an entire week, he claims I've won something. Get the fuck outta here with that bullshit.

Only Jesus knows how badly I want to fuck him right now.

The cursor is practicing voodoo on me, hypnotizing me with each black flash. It's like a neon sign pointing to the space where my thoughts are supposed to go. I could write a book about us there. I should've blocked his screen name instead of just deleting it. But then he wouldn't *know* I was ignoring him, and none of this would count. He has to see nyCALIgrl4 in bold letters at the top of his buddy list and realize that she hasn't IM'd him in days and that she probably never will again!

The cursor keeps blinking.

"It's like that McDonald's game, dude. Monopoly. Nobody ever wins that shit," says Gi, snapping me back to bitch and snatching my pointer, middle, and ring fingers away from the J, K, and L keys.

"Yeah, man," I concede in an exhale. But who loses? Have I lost if I leave this skinny blinking bitch alone and never find out what I've already won? Or do I win if I do what I (what all of us) always do: keep it the fuck moving? I take a minute to stare at the cursor, to stare at my idle fingertips, to stare at my magical keys, to stare at virtual Dex. And then I ex out of "IM with nycaligrl4 from Dex10" and hope he knows how hard that was.

It's three weeks until I turn twenty-eight, so three weeks and two years before I hit thirty and my face melts off. It's been one week since I started my online campaign against Dex10, five months since we broke up in real life, and four days since I met this new guy with a cleft chin, so it's who-knows-how-long before my next nonrelationship. Call me Kiefer: my life has been operating on a ticking-time-bomb scenario for the past year.

"Dude, what is your life about?!" quizzes Gina every morning over IM like the opening bell of a boxing match, startling me into the ring of another Monday. The alarm to starting the day off single.

"Ummmm, who the hell knows?" I say, too exhausted to think of anything better.

I don't feel almost twenty-eight. Not an actual adult, I'm more adult-*ish*. See, I'm just a girl. An awesome one, of course, but just one. And like so many other little brown girls my age, I believe the problem of loving, lusting, or even "liking liking" someone can be solved with a simple equation: $x + y =$ gtfohwtbs (if "x" ≥ 28 years old and "y" = socially retarded men). So when Dex10

IM's me again, I react as if on autopilot because doing otherwise would be to go against nature. I'm just following orders:

Dex1O (3:14:46 p.m.):	hey
nyCALIgrl4 (3:15:06 p.m.):	what?
Dex1O (3:15:26 p.m.):	oh
nyCALIgrl4 (3:16:14 p.m.):	is there something specific you wanted? or . . .
Dex1O (3:16:50 p.m.):	why are you asking so many questions? i was saying hello
nyCALIgrl4 (3:18:56 p.m.):	k
Dex1O (3:19:42 p.m.):	am i on death silence?
nyCALIgrl4 (3:20:02 p.m.):	ummm
nyCALIgrl4 (3:20:16 p.m.):	i dont really have anything to say to you
nyCALIgrl4 (3:20:21 p.m.):	have a nice life?
Dex1O (3:20:42 p.m.):	oh . . .

I'm *such* a badass. I am literally the baddest bitch on the planet. If there was a bitch contest between me and every other heartbroken, hissing, red-eyed, puffy-faced woman in the world, I would defeat every last one of them—handily. People should start worshipping me. To that end, I've prepared a few imaginary lectures on the subject of bitching yourself out of a relationship: Step 1, treat him as you would a tardy Comcast guy after waiting from 2:00 p.m. to 8:00 p.m.: with zero emotion save thinly sliced loathing . . .

Yeah, I don't believe me either. I'm a bitch, but I swear I don't want to be. Really, I think I have to be.

◇◇◇◇◇◇

What I really want is to grab this man and hold on for dear life, despite the fact that he kissed another girl in a club—more on that later—and told me I was too perfect for him and that he liked me as "more than a friend but less than a girlfriend." Cognitive dissonance, he called it. I want that blinking cursor to crap out all the words I'm thinking but not writing and turn that white space black like my heart. I want to see him naked again—just once. I want to make him eggs again.

I want never to be in love again.

To make sure I don't backslide, I copy, paste, and send my badass response to Gina. The two of us do some preprogrammed LOLing, WTFing, GTFOHing, and I feel encouraged—for now.

But what about later? If I lose this round, will there ever be another? I've wasted countless work hours Googling "marriage babies black" because, really, what's the point in finishing an article on the popularity of Sen. Clinton's pantsuits when I've been sentenced to a closet full of 'em. According to data from the U.S. Census bureau, in 2001 nearly 42 percent of black women over 15 years old (which I guess is marrying age now) had never been married, compared to 21 percent of white women the same age. Since 1970, the overall marriage rate in the U.S. has declined by 17 percent. For blacks, it's dropped 34 percent.

I hate math—and acronyms.

Never heard of the AAHMI? Me neither. The African American Healthy Marriage Initiative is sponsored by the Department of Health and Human Services. It has a Web site (although it's at a ".net," which is considerably less convincing than an ".org") and one hundred followers on Twitter. All those people get to hear its good news, like the fact that black families are less likely to be

5

headed by a married couple than any other ethnic group: 46 percent of black families "versus" 81 percent of all the others. Black families are also more likely to be headed by a single woman—45 percent of black families versus 14 percent for whites—and these manless women are popping out babies like it's going out of style. Sixty-eight percent of live births in our community are to unmarried women.

So, it's our stats *versus* the rest of the country's, and there's no time to go to the cards for a decision. It's over. Technical knockout. While our women were snatching up college degrees and busting up glass ceilings, our men were getting snatched up and busted. We were dreaming of them and waking up alone.

Well, not alone alone—remember, I've got an alarm clock.

◇◇◇◇◇◇

"Dude?"

"Dude."

This is how Gina and I say our hellos: *Dude. Dude? Dude, what the fuck. I don't know, dude. Duuuuude. Dude, yes!* We've known each other since back when I was lying about getting my period. I've been in love with her—no homo—since the eighth grade. This is my longest and most serious relationship. In fifteen years, she's never said, "Hey, it's Gina." I'd probably hang up if she did.

God, fifteen years makes us sound old as shit, doesn't it? I know, I know. At twenty-seven and counting, we're not really old old, but damn it, tell that to our uteruses (uterun, uteri?). Tell it to our mothers, who want grandchildren so badly they can catch a whiff of crappy diapers in the night air. Tell it to our fathers, whose abandonment is finally creeping up our throats with last night's Corona and grenadine. Tell it to our hearts that are so tired of being broken that they'd rather stay that way than be fixed for a better smashing later. I'm telling you, it's been rough—sorta.

I mean, we're not spinsters, quite yet. But still. Our age is measured in accomplishments now, not years. Five hundred twenty-five thousand six hundred minutes? More like five degrees, twenty-five boyfriends, six hundred Manolos. Marriage and babies? Waiter? At first I wanted both after my thirties, which according to *Sex and the City* were going to totally rock. But then I saw the movie, and those chicks looked wrinkly as hell.

Gina says she wants marriage before her eggs dry up—quote, end quote. The likelihood of her freezing them comes closer with each relationship gone bad. If whoever is acting right, the eggs are safe. Acting up? Then she Googles "cryogenics" plus "embryos" while giving me a lecture on advanced uterine aging. I want to tell her that our eggs *and* our hearts will be just fine. But I've never lied to her (except for that one time in 1994 when I pretended to have cramps).

"I'm on sabbatical from these dudes, man." She sounds halfway serious this time. "I need a break."

"Ummm, dude, you already know I feel you on that." I want to say something cheesy like the white girls do: *Some guy is going to realize how awesome and beautiful and wonderful you are and then everything will be great and you'll have a wedding and a baby and a house and a life and . . .*

"They're messing my whole life up," she says again a few weeks later while we're in a cab on our way back to my new "luxury" apartment. I've got door*men*—they work across the street, though, in North Face uniform jackets, and take super long breaks whenever the cops come around. When we slide out the cab heels first, they study us from their posts. We ignore the "compliments" they chip in on the dresses meant to entice better men. "Sex-zay," they sing in canon. One swipe of my security key and we're safe.

Right now it's September in Washington, which means the annual legislative conference of the Congressional Black Caucus is in town. The CBC is to single-black-chick Washington as Fleet Week is to single-white-gal New York. Seamen? How 'bout degreed men! "Dude, I will be out there for the menses," Gina e-mails in advance of flying four hours to spend half as many days scouring the capital city for the new American dream (political husband, professional wife, perfect children). We hurdled one party after another, double-daring ourselves to find someone worth the Spanx.

Really, the whole weekend was an exercise in corporal punishment. The highlights: One guy told me I had "award-winning calves," then handed me his business card. Sweet but fat. Another asked me what I did for a living, and then before I could answer, he slipped me *his* card, which read "sartorial artist" in the fancy letters that should be reserved for wedding invites. *Dude, he's a seamstress.* Next! Then a friend, who starred in more than a few of my mental pornos, showed up with his jeans *tucked into* combat boots. *He's gay, right? No!* I gave serious googly eyes to a few other prospects who gave me the side eye in return. Gina gave her number to some dude I said was a dork. *And?* I stared at the back of his egg-shaped head for a few seconds, mentally compelling him to call her on Monday. He didn't.

The rest of our nights were spent pointing out who was gay (everybody), and then the weekend was over. Now we're headed home alone with each other.

It's practically scientific how hyped one gets before a night out—all hopped up on *New Kids* and Corona—and then how quickly hope deflates. We say it's because we're getting too old for the club, but I swear it's because we're just bored of it. Plus, my feet hurt. Why's there never any place to sit the hell down?

Gina is staring out the window of her discontent as we drive up Rhode Island Avenue, lost in thought. I'm twenty-eight, she says, breaking the silence of a night that produced more bunions than love connections. This shit isn't a fucking game anymore, she says. I'm fucking tired, she says. It's two thousand and fucking eight, she says. I say Umm-hmm and look out my own window, wondering when and having no answers. We go the rest of the way in silence, drag ourselves up four flights, and fall asleep. Tomorrow, maybe, will be different.

◇◇◇◇◇◇

Lisa Nowak taught us different the year before.

"Please tell me you saw this shit about this crazy-ass white lady? The astronaut lady?" she IM'd me one morning as I clicked between the *New York Times* and TheYBF.com, pretending to bone up on Sen. Whoeverthehell's latest bill about scratching balls while scrolling through snark-infested blogs about black celebs and/or crazy white ladies.

So of course I'd seen it. Mug shots? Murderous monkey-junk love? A productive workday's worst nightmare. This was what the two of us lived for—something so ridiculous it warranted research.

"Fock! That shit was so damn awesome," I typed back. "I can't even breathe right now it's touching my heart so much."

"YES!!"

"Dude? Yes!"

And with that, a diapered astronaut became our muse—the awesome crazy we measured our own bizarre love lives against. If we didn't go *that* nuts (950 miles with Depends at the ready) over some dude with helmet hair, then maybe we'd be okay. Just maybe. This was the same year that we'd decided to stop "dating" and start "looking." Two thousand and seven was the year we officially entered our late twenties—the starting line of the death march to menopause. This was the year I fell in love with Dex10, Gina got proposed to, and we both came up smelling like teen spirit—overbored, in denial, and mostly unintelligible. Hello? It was the year my mother, a pot-smoking lesbian who in a moment of overbonding told me she'd been celibate for twelve years because she hadn't found "an acceptable mate," began to sneak "grandbabies" into every conversation. She even asked me to come visit her in Atlanta one bitter February.

"How do you know I don't have plans, like for Valentine's Day or something?"

"Well," she purred, "do you?"

I hate her sometimes.

This was also the year Gina erratically swore off black guys for white guys, then Jewish guys, then any guy, even gay guys. It was a flag on the play year for all of us girls. One of my best friends from home, Monique, was dating a married man with four kids who made $490 every two weeks.

"He's getting divorced."

"Yeah, but he *is* married now, right?"

She also had an on/off thing with this Sunday-jazz-brunch guitarist guy. We called him *Mr.* Damon because he was in his mid-forties, and we respect our elders. Two of my sorority sisters were getting divorces. They had three years of marriage and as many kids between them. My college roommate, Stella, was living with a potentially gay man and constantly checking his e-mail. She'd come across a few juicy tidbits—drinks with an ex when he was supposed to be with the guys—but I don't think she ever found what she was looking for.

This year, we had a certain refrain committed to memory: "Dude, where are the men at?" Gina would start.

"Sheeeeeeiiiiiit," I'd say. They might as well have been on the moon.

Our astronaut, Lisa Nowak, was like us. She was well educated: U.S. Naval Academy Class of 1985. She was successful: umm, NASA. And she would do practically anything to hold on to what she thought was a good man—checking his e-mail, Google-mapping her competition's whereabouts, then showing up unannounced. We worshipped her. The police found her in an airport parking lot in possession of a steel mallet, a four-inch buck knife, a BB gun, and a map to the home of her rival, Colleen Shipman. All Lisa wanted to do was "talk."

"Dude, if by 'talk' you mean do intense bodily harm!"

We laughed and cried over dirty astronaut diapers for months, dissecting every new morsel of the three-way between Nowak, Bill Oefelein, and Colleen, the other woman. This part was especially hilarious: while planning a vacation to his parents' home, Bill e-mailed Colleen to say that they needed a hotel room "due to noise requirements." He wrote, "We need some 'privacy'!!!!"

"Dude, why are there so many exclamation points in this correspondence?" I wrote.

"You KNOW he holding something," wrote back Gina.

"Grodie!"

We were diaper-dope sick, every day wondering if there was no end to what a hard-up housewife would do for a little romance— trash your current marriage, murder your coworker, crap your pants. But this was more than just another Midwest meltdown or celebrity slipup. Something besides the random ridiculousness of Nowak's situation made us hungry for her canonization. See, I don't watch *Flavor of Love*, *I Love New York*, *For the Love of Ray*

J, or *Real Chance of Love* because I like to keep my white people crazy limited to the Fox News Channel. So what kept us glued to Ms. Nowak wasn't just the fact of her lunacy—tune in to any of the aforementioned shows, and your eyes will bleed reality-TV red—but the *cause* of it. It was the same thing that was causing ours. When being interrogated by the police, Lisa described her fling with Bill as "more than a working relationship, but less than a romantic relationship." We immediately started a blog in her honor. Our mission statement:

> We here at Dirty Astronaut Diapers worship secretly at the altar Nowak. We send her the burnt offerings of all the failed relationships, blind dates, missed connections, and random hookups we've endured over our decade of dating—the epic saga we hope will one day lead, Odysseus-style, to marriage. Anyone who'll drive countless hours with a carload of latex gloves, black wig, trench coat, drilling hammer, rubber tubing, and about $600 to "talk" to the bitch who stole her man is a goddess among lesser women. So this is for you, Ms. Nowak—nay, this is for all you women out there who've been in "more than a working relationship but less than a romantic relationship."

I was obsessed with the blog for about a month—paying $29.99 for the domain name dirtyastronautdiapers.com, getting some college geek I found on Craigslist to design our Web site, and coming up with a pseudonym for my snarky but sentimental posts. Then we posted like three things on there and got bored of it. Hello, real life was calling. Plus, writing about how much our reality was biting seemed less like some type of postfeminist protest journal and more like a defeatist's dying declaration.

Remember that one scene in *SATC* when Carrie wants to go live in Paris with Petrovsky's old light-installing ass and Miranda's all, "What about your column?!" and Carrie's all, "I'm old as shit and I need to live my life instead of just writing about it for some bootleg tabloid nobody's heard of!" Sorta like that.

Still, sweet heavenly Jesus if we didn't know what it was like to be in the more than / less than emotional equation—who *doesn't* know what that's like? Stuck in that in-between place where nobody's happy, nobody's leaving, and everyone thinks you're settling. But as black women, we felt an even bigger gravitational pull toward the jerks who were at once unworthy and seemingly worthwhile (and I speak for all black women because I can). How many times had we convinced ourselves of someone else's potential while ignoring our own, giving each other great advice that we never follow (girl, he just might not be right for *you*)?

Crazy astronaut ladies and fabulous twenty-something black chicks are in the same spaceship: they're aliens among men blasting off to who knows where.

Right before we met Lisa, I'd just finished licking the wounds of a wasted year being way more than a friend but much less than a girlfriend to a Wellbutrin-popping Muslim podiatrist named Abdul. I slipped up once and said something about "this relationship" in casual conversation. "What relationship?" he asked. Abdul was preceded by West Point Willy, who drunk-dialed a proposal that he, of course, couldn't recall the next morning. I pretended not to care. Then came possibly gay Winston, two-timing Darin, crazy Darin, short Eddie, possibly gay Jean Claude, etc., etc., etc.

Also, I had been surviving the workday by Facebook-stalking James, a summer associate in my job's legal department, whom

I fell in love with during a seminar on libel. He was staring at me so hard, my white work wife passed me a note: "That guy is totally checking you out!" No shit, Sherlock. He sneezed a few times during said meeting, so afterward I slipped him a packet of raspberry lemonade Emergen-C. He asked me out to Starbucks the next day.

"Soooo, basically this cat is an intern," said Gina, doing her best to sound supportive.

James and I played relationship limbo for a while, meeting for coffee and philosophy twice a week and hooking up once in his bedroom, which was missing a door because it was two-timing him with the better half of a living room. A week later, he told me we couldn't get "romantically involved" because it might affect him professionally. Dude, you're a fucking intern! You've got Ikea curtains for walls! Six months later, I was still convinced we could make it work. I mean, he grew up in Namibia and France and Arkansas. Barack and Michelle 2.0!

At my twenty-seventh birthday party, about a year after the Emergen-C move, I slunk over to where James was standing and wrapped my fingers around his bicep. "Soooo, what are weeeee doing later?"

"You mean after *this*?" He used his martini glass to draw a circle around the crowd.

"Yes, retard."

"Wait, you wanna have *sex*!"

"Omigod. I can't." We left shortly after and did.

That was also the first time I met Dex10 (also known as Dexter). I don't remember it (James, champagne, hormones), but supposedly I was extremely friendly.

"Dude, get your fucking life together," was the message that came down from the Oracle. But then again, she was the one who'd spent the past three years "dating" a guy we called the

Fireman because he was a fireman. He wanted to marry her and move her to St. Louis, where he fought fires and stuff. "I'm too bourgie for that shit," was her answer. So now she's playing red light / green light with Bilal, who thinks marriage is for suckers and children are unethical.

The point is, we're becoming *those* women. The ones guys refer to as "wifey material," since apparently spouses come in specific fabric grades. After about a week of flirting online, Dex10 described me this way: "Hi, my name's Helena and I'm awesome. The end." Gee, thanks. I'll make sure to keep that in mind when we break up for the fifty thousandth time. Suddenly, Lisa Nowak didn't look so crazy. Actually, she might have been on to something.

What does "wifey material" even mean when someone at the *Washington Post* thinks the headline "Marriage Is for White People?" is okay? The article, of course, became another one of Gina's and my obsessions. The *Washington* fucking *Post* was against us now.

"Dude, is there anyone out there who wants us to find a man?" I asked, more begging than wondering. SOSing, really.

"Nope."

The reporter who wrote the story worked part-time with kids, who I'm going to assume were from the "inner city," because those are the kids people write about in newspapers. Once, in one of her classes, during a discussion on how to be a good father, one frustrated little boy said, "Marriage is for white people," and clearly a movement was born (remember the AAHMI? Me neither). This kid wasn't into the whole "first comes love, then comes marriage, then comes the baby in the baby carriage" thing. Perhaps Nursery Rhymes that Subliminally Teach Minority Children about Healthy Social Institutions 101 should be a kindergarten requirement.

If so, Dexter would still be eating Play Doh, instead of just playing dumb. Fast-forward to a scene between my sheets on one of the many horrendously long Saturday nights that led to my ignoring him on IM.

So, we're naked and he goes, "I don't know. It's like . . . I don't know . . . Maybe it's that I don't think I can live up to the low expectations you have of me." He's looking past my forehead.

"What?" I'm trying to sound as nonmurderous as possible. No such luck. "Are you fucking serious right now? Like are you actually saying this to me right now?"

"Helena, you're the most amazing person." Now he's looking me in the eyes. "Like, I'll never meet anyone better than you. I just know I'll mess this up." He was slipping through my fingers, and I couldn't clench my fists fast enough. It was one of those terrifying, long-winded, up-late, naked conversations that never begin or end. The first of many we'd have.

This particular cram session all started with a bad fashion choice.

I'd "caught" Dexter—at this point my maybe-boyfriend for at least a month—kissing some girl in a club. Yep, he was tonguing down some light-skinned, curly-haired, Forever XXI fashion-top-wearing girl. The shirt she had on was asymmetrical. Repeat. He kinda betrayed me with a girl wearing a shirt that was long-sleeved on one side and tube top on the other. After a marathon curse-out, he managed to make the situation not about his "cheating"—we weren't exclusive yet—but about my inherent awesomeness physically compelling him to treat me like "some stupid chick off the fucking street," in my humble opinion.

Was I too perfect? What kind of crazy monkey-junk logic was that? Was he just not that into me? Did I actually just ask myself that? What kind of maniac subscribes to a self-loathing brand of reasoning created by a comic with frosted tips? So what was it then? And we're back to the beginning. What would Lisa do? Where does one purchase a mallet?

We'd started out promisingly enough. Dex was terrifyingly good-looking and had a quirky I-write-poetry-about-the-women-I-date-to-make-each-one-feel-special thing going. He was in law school. He'd be my Cliff. And I'd be a less pathetic Pygmalion. James who?

Then, on that never-ending Saturday night, I stupidly decided to do a drive-by. Sure, I was going to check up on him at the club, but I was going to be super-covert about it—two-stepping in the background and pretending not to care about what he was doing over there with that woman dressed for Homecoming 1996. So the girls and I posted ourselves on the fringes of the dance floor, and he was so good for the first two hours.

Then I came back from the bathroom.

"Stop staring at him!" I screamed over the music. They were busy drilling neat holes in the back of Dex's head, arms crossed over their chests like pissed-off principals.

"That girl just kissed him," said Adrienne, my best friend since freshman year, too matter-of-factly to be joking.

"Ummm, what?"

"She kissed him on the lips," she repeated in the same "just the facts, ma'am" voice they use with victims on *SVU*. "We both saw it. There wasn't tongue or anything. But definitely on the lips. Whaddyawannado?"

What do I want to do? *What do I want to do?* I want to fucking scream is what I want to do! I want to punch that bitch in the damn throat and slap that shirt back to the bargain-basement bin to which it belongs. I want to slap *you* for seeing them tongue each other down and then telling me about it. I want to hop in my time machine and take back the blow job I gave him last night. Fock! This dude was supposed to be *it*. I took him to an office party, for Jesus' sakes. An office party! I couldn't stop saying, "Oh fuck." He was gorgeous and smart and funny and muscle-ly and beautifully weird and ugly when he came. I'd farted in front of him and didn't bother to pretend it wasn't me. And now I was going to have to start over. But fuck it, right? Keep it moving.

Yeah, maybe tomorrow morning.

I clicked over to where Dexter was sitting with Forever XXI girl and pounded my fingers into his left shoulder. "We need to fucking talk."

He was surprised to see me but followed my back through the club without asking questions. I pushed past people like an astronaut with space dementia. When I finally whirled around to face him, I could tell he was drunk. "Are you here with that fucking girl?" I screamed with my feet shoulder width apart and my nails digging into my hips. Power stance. "And don't even try to fucking lie, ass face, because Adrienne saw you licking her goddamn titties." Dex's eyes got big, but he didn't deny it, not even the parts I'd made up. Not a sound came out of this man's mouth, even though it was so wide open I could've put my fist through it. I thought seriously about doing that.

"Omigod, your breath! It's doing karate moves. Close your fucking mouth, retard!"

He closed it, and I left.

I ran past Adrienne, who'd witnessed my meltdown along with a bouncer and a few other people, to the ATM across the street to try and get $20 for a cab. Why do I never have cash?! Adrienne ran too. "Get in my car, Helena. I know you're embarrassed, but it's me, dude." Fock.

18

As soon as I got into my apartment, my always empty but now totally emptier apartment, I flipped open my laptop and deleted Dexter from Facebook, MySpace, AIM, and my Outlook address book. I needed to do something real. But really, he was just another ephemeral disappeared-into-the-Internet ether. Nothing. It was 4:00 a.m., and I wore down my living room floor pacing back and forth, making guttural sounds—grunting like a damn maniac because I couldn't cry. I *wouldn't* cry—not after only five weeks. So instead I lay on my bed, hissed at the ceiling through clenched teeth like a woman in labor, and waited for sleep to come.

Then he caaaaalled, and we taaaalked, and he beeeegged, and I liiiiistened.

Yes, I am totally familiar with how ridiculously pathetic I am. How fucked I am in this entire situation. How like Lisa I am right now. She'd been in outer space. Outer freaking space! I assume she knew she was better than dirty Depends (I mean, there *are* rest stops). And yet this woman, this woman who was like us in so many ways, was willing to abandon life on the moon for a man with whom she shared "more than a working relationship but less than a romantic relationship." Does success drive you totally insane? Or do men?

Six months and one Lisa later, I still didn't know for sure. This is why I can't answer Dex's whining IMs. This is why I *have* to get over him. This is why I've been super-strong and full of resolve for the past two weeks. This is why when I saw him walking up the stairs of yet another club just last night, my stomach flipped, my eyes went all watery, and I almost choked on a shard of ice. This is why when he came over to our pack with a shit-eating grin on his face and *embraced* one of *my* friends and then tried to give me the one-armed homie hug, I gave him the thumbs-up. This is why, when I saw him later the same night, this time standing by himself at the bar looking all lonely and irresistible like DVF at Filene's, I *had* to say hello. This is why we ended up talking all night. This is also why I woke up to him the next morning and have to start all over again with the whole ignoring thing.

This is why I never win.

GETTING MY HAIR UNDID

Know how I found out my family thought my mother was a crack-addicted sex fiend who dabbled in the international child slave ring and planned to sell her only daughter to the highest bidder? Over the phone and under a hair dryer.

"Whaaaa?"

"I never told you this?" Umm, no.

See, Frances does this. We'll be talking about something FCC-approved for mothers and daughters, like, say, vaginal itch, and she'll bust in like the emergency broadcasting system with a "What kind of birth control do you use?" or an "I've been celibate for almost a decade" or an "Oh, so you two are just fuck buddies then." Beeeeeeep goes the filial flat line. Dead. She's got mommy Tourette's.

Even better than talking, she'll actually *do* things that are totally unkeeping for a woman her age or sexual orientation. In a perfect world, I'd be blissfully oblivious to these random acts of kinkiness, but for the persistent photo evidence. It's as if she's leaving me Kodak crumbs, snapshot SOSes. Like the time I found a picture of her with Treach. Yes, that Treach, one half of the Grammy-winning rap duo Naughty by Nature, who famously asked, "Ya down with O.P.P.?"

"What. The hell. Is this?" I say, ripping the four-by-six from her fridge and eyeing it up close. Oh, it's Treach, all right. I pinch a triangle of the edge and dangle it in her direction.

"Oh yeah, he's a performer," she says, actually using the word *performer*, which proves just how wrong it is for her to be in this picture.

"Jesus, woman!" I feign a proper degree of daughterly disgust, when really I'm proud of how utterly ridiculous she is. How totally unacceptable her whole life is. She's in this picture cheesing like someone told her to, holding a glass of champagne, and wearing Treach's arm for a shawl. This lady is old enough to be *wearing* shawls. According to her version of the night in question, the two of them—my mommy and the hip-hop star—just happened to be in the same club celebrating the release of a porno Treach was in—she claims ignorance here—and Frances, being Frances, finagled her way into VIP bottle service, because that's what she does. Now she's got proof of how inappropriate she is magnetically fixed to her fridge.

It was also through *This Week in Pictures: The Frances Andrews Edition* that I learned she'd gotten married. I was in grad school at the time, and the "wedding" to which I did not receive an invitation had taken place a few months before. The groom was this African guy named Isa, who was gay and illegal. Frances wore garb for the "ceremony," which in five-by-seven looked like it took place in the kind of church basement slash community center slash banquet hall in which fake marriages are held. Less than two years later, they were found out by the Feds when neither one could remember (a) the last time they had sex or (b) which way the toilet paper rolled off the handle. Frances said two weeks ago and under. Isa said two months ago and over. The INS agent decided to be merciful and file their interview in a trash can. Better it never existed.

Frances is an oxymoron personified. She grows ganja next to her geraniums and "Gee milacres!" is her go-to exclamation. She thinks having a nice pair of "slacks" is synonymous with success but will never set foot in a mall and whines whenever you ask her to try something on. Ikea is her Shangri-la, but every piece of furniture she owns was "found" on somebody's curb. She has absolutely no clue what O.P.P. stands for but has a seemingly endless catalog of original-score birthday songs. When I turned twenty-eight, she sang a new one to my voice mail. And I thought I'd heard 'em all.

> *Blowing out the candles on my birthday cake,*
> *my birthday cake, my birthday caa-ake.*
>
> *Blowing out the candles on my birthday cake,*
> *I'm another year old to-day.*
>
> *Blowing out the candles on my birthday cake,*
> *my birthday cake, my birthday day caa-ake.*
>
> *Blowing out the candles on my birthday cake,*
> *and when I do a wish I'll maa-aake.*
>
> *Blowing out the candles on my birthday cake,*
> *I'm another year old to-day.*

On this Saturday morning over the drone of the hair dryer, her voice is just as clear, cutting through the metal hood like a cake knife when she says, "Oh yeah, Grandmommy and Auntie and all them thought I was going to sell you on the black market in Spain. They thought I was on crack." Since I'm in the beauty salon and not an insane asylum, screaming is out of the question.

◇◇◇◇◇◇

When we were six and thirty-five, Frances decided to move us to Madrid. We were living in Lancaster then, a place Californians refer to as the high desert, not to be confused with the low desert, which doesn't exist to my knowledge, or is otherwise known as Los Angeles, the city Frances and I are technically from.

She never once sat me down to explain why we were becoming expats—if we were running away or toward something. All I know is that one day we were settled in "a two-story house with snow" (my personal request), and the next we were in a constant state of moving—selling my Snoopy scooter and giving away the wild horse she bought me for my birthday. She never framed it as a question like they do on 1950s sitcoms: *Hey, Little Ricki, how'd ya like to go to Cuba?*

We moved allllll the time. And by all the time, I'm not using the suburban kid pejorative where moving maybe once or twice in one's little lifetime is so soul-crushing and eventful that one grows up wanting to be established and home-owning. No, I mean we moved whenever she felt like it, and because everything she felt meant everything to me, moving became our secret game. Secret in that only I knew the rules, so technically every time I won.

If I came home from school, and Frances said, "Guess what?" I didn't immediately start searching the house for a new Cabbage Patch Kid. I knew the score. With this woman, a "guess what" wasn't an invitation to imagine; it was a prerequisite for packing. In place of "Guess what? Ground chuck was 39 cents off today. Tacos!" I got "Guess what? The dollar is way up. Learn Spanish!"

I wasn't scarred by it or anything—at least not in the beginning. 'Cause see, I liked moving. Loved it, actually.

Then came the trip to Spain that went terribly wrong, forever ruining our secret game.

I don't have a childhood home—but homes. There does not exist in the greater Los Angeles area any street whose name I recall, whose sidewalks I hear, whose air I can taste, but it's okay, because I've got the flash cards. These quick-flipping images that, when sorted through, give me some idea of what being Frances's "first and last" was like.

There are two piles. The first has all the places I sort of remember—a brownish green yard and a black puppy that got away; another puppy found limp with his nose in a box of Abba-Zabas; a porcelain bathtub I pooped in while there was water in it; a pink corduroy jumper decorated in the front with throw-up because Frances left me with strangers without saying good-bye; a crumpling Victorian mansion filled with "special" people to whom she gave pills and to whom I gave orders; a red Porsche at night with the top down.

The second pile has all the places I can see clearly. My favorite is the street with our white wooden house and the steepled church on the corner. Dressed up like a clown, I celebrated my fifth birthday in that backyard. Or I could've had on a grass skirt made out of discarded palm tree leaves or a thrift-shop trench coat cut up to look like Inspector Gadget's—whatever, costume is every late October baby's burden. In the kitchen there was a cot I slept on not because there wasn't an extra bedroom, but because refrigerator noises were so scary that being close to them helped me fall asleep. Made sense then.

My best friend was another little girl named Jocelyn, who lived three houses down. She had a beautiful older brother and a huge clubhouse/refrigerator box in her backyard.

We shared everything, me and Jocelyn—an obsession with "doing it," the lyrics to "Let's Hear It for the Boys," ingenious blueprints for the refrigerator box, and . . . urine. In some clairvoyant preparation for our futures in nightclub bathrooms, we always peed at the same time. Like, literally. Both our bony butts could fit on one toilet seat simultaneously. We tested this once as a joke or dare—I can't remember which—and decided to stick with it. It was both economical and efficient. Mine on one side and hers on the other, our cheeks barely touching. I doubt anyone knew we were pee-pee partners or even cared. Still, we thought we were doing something nasty, something significant.

As if on cue Frances announced our third move in a year right when me and Jocelyn had a good rhythm going, a pissy symphony if you will. This time it was to somewhere called Lancaster—a two-hour drive up north. She said Jocelyn could come visit if she wanted. I shrugged; synchronized urination wasn't so complicated that it couldn't be duplicated with someone else. The new Jocelyn (whoever that might be) would do, because Jocelyn was just the new somebody else and so on and so on—a funhouse mirror of best friends. This was during my "me" phase—do phases last twenty-seven years?—so every one of our moves meant just one thing to me. Well, a few things: new stuff, new Jocelyns, new pets, a new car, definitely a new school, and, of course, the new Helena.

Supposedly she chose Lancaster because months before I'd put in a special request for a house with stairs and snow, so in mumbo-jumbled reverse psychology terminology the uprooting of our lives for the fifty-thousandth time was really all *my* decision. ME! Permission to start decades of self-fascination? Granted.

There were three other black kids in our row of town houses. Frances was like the manager of our apartment home community or something. We were living the high life—hello, stairs—

and as far as I could tell, we were now not only rich but also famous. Or at least I was. I made sure everyone saw me skating in the backyard parking lot with my new purple Barbie skates, not noticing they were on the wrong feet until Frances pointed it out; that everyone saw me scooting fluently on my pink-tasseled Snoopy scooter, which I'd been prescribed due to my bike-riding phobia; that everyone knew I had a snapping turtle named Tyrone, but not that I tortured him with sharpened pencils.

Existing exclusively in my own head, I collected best friends like My Little Ponies but was happiest alone. Common household items were my real friends—black markers, fingernail files, hairbrushes, red plastic cups, left shoes, bitten-off pencil erasers, power cords, matted toothbrushes, untwisted paper clips. They were all characters in my inanimate soaps. *Why should I buy you Barbies when you'd rather play with school supplies?* "The Numbers" was one melodrama mentally rewound so often I'm surprised the tape kept working. See, 3 and 4 were the elderly parents of 5, who was good and sweet and desperately in love with 6, the innocent beauty who herself was in love with 7 and never realized her secret power over 9, the billionaire brat who was betrothed to 8, who, of course, kept herself busy plotting against 6 and lusting after 7. I can't remember what 1 and 2 did. Directed, probably.

There was this one time when Frances, anticipating an early start the next morning, trusted me to get myself up and ready for school. A second-grader reading on a fourth-grade level, I awoke feeling so over it. What was all the fuss about? I'd be fine. Picked out a white sundress paired with purple snow boots because it was January.

This was also the same day I "forgot" to wear panties. Flowy dress, meet the wind. Wind, meet my tiny bare ass cheeks. Why six-year-old me decided to go grade-school commando escapes me. If I had to guess, somehow underwear seemed unnecessary. When I met up with the kids that lived a few doors down to walk to school, nobody said nothing.

It was as if I'd been dressing like a Russian child prostitute all my life. School pictures were that day. The A's, being down in front, were given the star treatment, totally unmissable. Unfortunately, sitting Indian-style, so was my hoo-ha. Mrs. What's-her-guts couldn't wait to dime me out to Frances. Jerk. Apparently there was a seasonally appropriate pink sweat suit waiting blatantly on the downstairs couch that I'd completely missed in my rush to be grown.

Mrs. What's-her-guts, stool pigeon that she was, had a bunch more to report: I'd been cheating on our class book assignment for months—tracing my mother's signature on the "how many pages I read today" thingy she sent home every week. Plus, I frequently erased myself from the chalkboard reserved for naughty names; plus, I cheated at Heads Up Seven Up; plus, I was sneaking unauthorized Sprite into my lunch canister and telling people it was water. Needless to say, I never saw my legs or the light of day again that winter, and when the subject of moving to Spain came up, I was hardly in a position to whine it down.

"Do they have *Fraggle Rock?*" Watching singing mole men construct a never-finished underground maze of scaffolding was my only prerequisite for flying around the world with her.

"Yes, little brown-eyed girl, they've got everything in Spain," she said, playing piano on my ribs as I stood accusing her in our kitchen—the first we'd had with a dishwasher. I wouldn't let myself laugh or give her the satisfaction of knowing I'd follow her anywhere.

"Is it in *Spanish?*" I asked, slumping down to the floor away from her tickling fingers, realizing that our lives would always be like this: move here, move there, move here, move there.

"Yes." She didn't sound defeated. She knew she was abominable.

"Then I don't wanna go," I said, fingering the grooves between the tiles on the floor. This was one of the first real house-houses that we'd ever lived in. She had a real job. I'd gone to the same school for almost an entire grade. She'd bought me a wild pony that I never rode once because, umm, it was wild, but I loved it fiercely. We kept Misty, named after a cousin I barely saw, at a stable not too far from our house-house. At six, I was finally ready to be settled, and here she was once again, all too ready to be restless.

I got back at her by fixating on my death, constantly asking Frances what she would do when I died suddenly in my sleep or crossing the street to school. The countdown to Spain became a macabre advent calendar with questions about my imminent demise decorating each new day. If I didn't ask about her life without me, I thought it might come that much sooner.

"What would you do if I died tomorrow?"

"Oh, I don't know, little brown-eyed girl."

"I'm serious! What would happen?"

"I don't know. I'd probably gather up all your pictures and your clothes and your toys and I'd move way up in the mountains somewhere." Good answer, lady. Because if I didn't exist, then she couldn't either. More than a package deal, we were Siamese. Maybe Spain wasn't such a crappy idea after all. We'd disappear together. Like old times.

Or maybe not. In the end, my second-grade OCD couldn't save us.

Obviously there was a lot of packing and preparation in the months leading up to our escape, but me being six and totally self-absorbed, I remember none of this. Alls I know is that one day we were in the desert, and the next, we were on the 405

Freeway trying to get to LAX with my grandmother in the driver's seat. It was just the three of us, waiting with the rest of the cars to get to our respective point B's. Sitting in traffic, I watched an accident on the shoulder through a frame made with my thumbs and pointer fingers. There was an ambulance, a mangled car, and a stretcher covered with a white sheet. *No bueno.* Convinced that whatever was underneath was dead, I held my breath because breathing suddenly felt like bragging. I squatted up to the window and watched from the backseat of my grandmother's Nissan, trying not to choke on her cigarette smoke.

"Lena, sit back." She was a barker. Effie, my mother's mother, is the type of grandmother who'd rather give an order than a cookie. I loved her because I knew she could break me if she really wanted to. And most times I imagined she did want to. I admired her restraint.

Without protest, I sat back down on my butt and shoved myself as far back into the upholstery as possible, craning my neck to see the coffin on wheels being rolled into the ambulance. Nobody seemed to care. I closed my eyes and smoked a secondhand Virginia Slim.

At the airport, I waited in the car while Frances got out to handle the whole checking-in-to-move-your-only-child-halfway-around-the-world-for-God-knows-what process, which surprisingly didn't take long at all. Commanded to be still, I followed her with my eyes like a haunted-house portrait. See Frances waiting in line. See Frances at the ticket counter. See Frances handing someone some papers. See Frances smiling. See Frances waving.

She motioned to me from inside, giving me the international hand sign for "Get out of the car and come start the rest of your life!" I could have sworn I saw her mouth those words, so I jumped to put my fingers on the handle.

"No, Lena, stay," rasped Effie from the driver's seat, not even bothering to turn around or even eye me from the car mirror. She hadn't said much more than "Umm-hmm" since the accident. The sudden presence of her voice made the car almost claustrophobic. Only she could make "stay" sound like a complete sentence. There was no question of obedience. This was the woman whose number my mother made me repeat like a prayer of protection whenever I went somewhere alone—Girl Scout camp, sleepovers, down the street. *You okay, little brown-eyed girl?* Yes. *What's Grandmommy's number?* 779-7520! *Good girl.* So with one syllable I sat back in my seat and looked straight ahead, ignoring my mother, who was standing alone waiting for me.

Then we drove off.

◇◇◇◇◇◇

After however long it takes to get away with stealing someone, my grandmother dropped me off at the house of an unfamiliar and hugely fat old woman I'd never seen before, except for maybe in my nightmares. Truthfully, she was perfectly nice, but still— hello, I had been kidnapped!

Grandmommy said I'd be staying with Mrs. Humongobutt (as my memory calls her now) for some adult-sanctioned and therefore indeterminate amount of time. She also said that my mother was going on ahead to Spain without me. That's when I knew this was all bullshit. That nothing was going as planned. Because I knew us. Me and Frances, we were forever. That's when I decided not to run. She'd be coming for me. I don't even remember shedding more than two or three tears, and those were just for show. Didn't want them to suspect anything. She *was* going to come for me—eventually, maybe.

Swaddled in a muumuu on most days, Mrs. H made me feel more houseguest than hostage. I remember her gray hair, parted in four parts and then braided into thick ropes the length of ChapStick. Her granddaughter lived there too (or maybe she was brought in to keep me company), and the two of us played while she was cooking, which was always. Her granddaughter was no new Jocelyn, but prisoners can't be picky. Her name was something like LaNiece or Michelle. Whatever, she's barely important—actually, that's not right. Without her constant distractions—it was at Humongobutt's that I learned you shouldn't lick toilets and to sing gospel—I would've had to think about where I was and where I wasn't. I was somewhere between alone and afraid. I wasn't learning my Espanish. When it was dark, I'd pretend to dream, but I spent most nights wide awake, imagining a plane with Frances in it flying over the roof. Straining my ears, listening for the once-frightening roar to turn into my mother's voice, like thunder before the possibility of lightning. After hours of waiting, I'd finally go to sleep, knowing she wasn't in the sky.

The five days I spent without a mother were and will always be the worst of my life. Frances was my dirt, and when she left, she took my feet with her. A six-year-old girl without gravity. Weightless but not flying, because that would have been a relief. Instead, I was in a constant state of losing—spending one minute remembering the plump of the small bump on both her pinkies where her sixth finger used to be, and the next minute trying to picture the curl of the three hairs near her chin. There were moments when I could call up her face on speed dial and others when I couldn't remember the number to save my life. I needed saving.

Repression was my refuge. There are few things I can remember from that week. Whose clothes did I wear? Where did I sleep? What did I eat? How did I cope? Why didn't I jump out a window? No one spoke of Frances to me, except once. According to Humongobutt, a glass of water cost like $5 in Spain, and apparently that was a lot and therefore more than my mother could afford. She said this by way of explaining my presence in her home. My grandmother, according to this woman I'd never met before, was saving me. A messiah, not a mobster. Also, according to this woman, because Frances had failed to calculate the exorbitant cost of drinking into our Spanish plans, she was therefore unfit not only as a mother but as a human being. *Your mother didn't know what she was getting you all into.* Plus, you know, she had just left me here all alone in an unfamiliar America like Fievel. I was better off now, supposedly. Nobody said she'd be back.

After spending about a week with Humongo and LaNiece-Michelle, a familiar face finally showed up. Without explanation—a recurring motif—my auntie Barbara came and took me away on a boat.

She was the youngest of my mother's four sisters, and I was in awe of her. She knew everything. She smelled like clean, shopped at Robinsons-May, and had a high-class voice that made me feel special. But when she came to spring me from Humongo's, I knew I hadn't been rescued yet. She took me to the mall, for McDonald's, and then to Catalina Island for a day at the beach with a bunch of skinny kids I'd never met. I ran, I jumped, I ate sand, I threw sand; I was a child finally. In the fleeting moments not crowded with activity, I felt guilty for all the fun being had sans Frances—but I needed this. Maybe this was my new life, I thought. Maybe from now on, I would be bounced from unknown to unfamiliar and then back to alone. Maybe I should just adjust.

After one day of feeling normal and loved, Auntie dropped me back off at Mrs. H's without explanation, and I went back to being a motherless child. Later she'd say that I seemed happy, well-adjusted. Her job, I think, was to make sure they—my grandmommy, Humongobutt, the Boogie Man—hadn't severely damaged me in some irreparable fashion. To see how I was, then report back to whoever masterminded this whole thing. These women were protecting me from something horrible, something they couldn't name, something Frances must not have known existed. Snapping my childhood in two was simply par for the course.

I figured it was really Frances they wanted tamed. I was just an irksome but unavoidable byproduct. No more panty-free days at school, no more moving on impulse, no more lesbians, no more living. That was the first time I cried, when Auntie left me on that fat woman's doorstep with a shopping bag full of new stuff and emptied-out insides. Even LaNieceMichelle couldn't shut me up. I remember well what it's like to be a child crying. The slobber, the spit, the throat-scratching stuttering and uncontrollable shoulders.

The old lady held me to her massive boobage for a long time, trying either to suffocate me or to give me succor. I wished she'd done the former.

I was captive for four, five days at the most. Then Effie, whom I hadn't seen or heard from since we sped away from the airport together, came and got me. Just like that. She didn't say where we were going or why. I grabbed the plastic bag with my new two-piece in it and climbed back into the getaway car from just a few days before. I didn't say good-bye to Humongo or LaNiece-Michelle. I never saw them again, and at six I knew that would be the case. We drove in smoky silence through L.A. smog. Me trying not to choke her with the strings of my bikini. Her eyeing me every once in a while from the car mirror. I knew where we were once we got to the brick alley that always led to the back of

Effie's house. She still wasn't talking, but I knew Frances was around here somewhere.

The car stopped. The engine cut off. A front door opened. I pulled a handle. I jumped to the concrete. I saw her.

Someone grabbed my arm, slapped a vein, and shot me up with Christmas morning, new puppy, the last day of school, and snow boots all at once. I ran to her, my arms flying open involuntarily, straining like ghost limbs for feelings that had been snatched away. Frances didn't make a sound. She dropped to her knees and let me smash into her chest. Whatever tears refused to come when I first lost her marched from my eyes, tiny soldiers on a steady and quiet advance down my cheeks. I put my hands on her face, pulling her skin to the right and left, making sure it was the real her under there and not a fake. I circled my arms around her neck, landed my ear between her breasts, closed my eyes, and listened. We rocked. Finally, after what seemed like forever, we would get up from the patch of grass. Frances suggested out loud that we take a walk around the block to get reacquainted. My grandmother nodded, and we left.

We were about halfway around the block when a van screeched up to the curb beside us, the side door slid open, and a man pulled me in. *You gotta be kidding me!* Thank God, Frances came too.

◇◇◇◇◇

I'd like to think we were to Catalina Island as Jesus will be to the Rapture—thieves in the night. That I was whisked to this secret place via some covert method of whisking from the big red boat that brought us there to the brown van that zipped up the street of Avalon to the twin beds of the Edgewater hotel, where I was finally settled. That we stole the souls of all the white, Christian, and blond, with her blackness and my ashy knees.

In real life, Frances and I arrived in broad-ass daylight. We walked the half mile to the hotel by the beach that would become our newest home. She carried the big bag, and I carried the small one. It knocked against my six-year-old thighs with every step I tried matching to hers, our shadows moving like one three-legged, lopsided monster.

That's how we ended up walking down Crescent Avenue in Avalon with only two bags. The small town on the small island was only twenty-six miles across the sea, but we might as well have been on the moon. This would be the start of my factual childhood, not the new Helena but the real one. Everything before it was a blessed blur—Jocelyn, Lancaster, Misty the pony, moving, kidnapping. Memories of this place had more weight than the six years that came prior—capture the flag in People's Park, sixth grade with Mrs. Paul, breeding Crystal the rabbit, my first drink at Descanso Beach, throwing peanuts on the floor of Antonio's, Bobby M.'s sandy blond hair. Little more than two thousand people lived on Catalina, most of them religious, all of them white. Frances and I increased the black population by 200 percent. Here we were memorable, and I remembered nothing from the previous us. We were technically from Los Angeles, but Catalina is where I originated.

"Really, sweet the beat? You've been here before?" Frances asked, probably tired from kidnapping her own daughter back from her own mother but still sounding interested.

"Yeah, over there." I pointed. "Auntie Barbara brought me, and she bought me a new *two* piece, and . . ." I told her the rest of my story but got no reaction. Umm, two pieces are a big deal. *Hellooooooo*. We walked the last piece of the way in silence, checked into a hotel, and went about the business of settling in. Finally.

We spent the next five and a half years on the island, still moving constantly, of course. But this time there wasn't far to go.

There was one public school, one post office, one Chinese food place, and two pizzerias called Antonio's. Whatever insanity we'd experienced to get there got swallowed up by the ocean.

Two decades later, through the blast of a hair dryer, I found out why.

What had happened was a grammatical error, a misinterpretation of synonyms. Before we left for Spain, one of my mother's ex-lovers asked if she was taking me along too. My mother replied, "Of course: Lena is my biggest asset." Frances had gotten a job as a nanny to a rich American family in Madrid. I'd be raised up with their kids, go to an international school, eat tapas, and be exotic. What Frances meant by "asset" was that I was like a prototype—the most important bullet point on her mommy résumé. This ex of hers thought that by "asset," Frances meant something more along the lines of goods for sale, the liquefiable kind. So then this asshole called up my grandmother, and my grandmother called my aunties, and my aunties called each other, and a few days later, Frances would end up alone in an airport parking lot. In a *really* crazy twist, my grandmother had my mother arrested. *So we were both in prison.* Frances could have me back, Effie promised, only after marrying a man named Herbert, staying in California, and raising me up right. After five days of stubbornness, she was freed and we sailed away.

I learned all this at the hair salon.

"And do you know Barbara and them never apologized?" Even with singed ears, I could hear the disappointment in her voice.

THE BEATITUDES OF
ST. CLAIR

It was in Catalina at the house on Whittley Avenue that I got the courage to ask her.

I was in sixth grade by then, with a head streaked blond by the summer and a soul that belonged to *The Cosby Show*. A bottle of Sun-In might've solved things—bleaching out the black and covering up the gay—but I wanted something more permanent for us.

Every Thursday at eight, I had an impossible choice—pedal up Country Club Road to hear parents-cum-preachers talk about how blessed we were to be saved so early, or have a night in with Cliff and Clair. Eternal damnation had never been so prime-time.

For almost two years I'd been going to Awana Club meetings with all the other kids who needed Jesus, memorizing Precious Moments Bible verses for a chance to win plastic crap with "Sparky points." "Awanas" is for parents who think Girl Scouts are the devil and juice boxes save. We met once a week at the K–12 and got brainwashed into believing. Every meeting began with the Awana official battle hymn, which goes, "Hail Awa-nas, marching for the youth (hey!) / Hail Awa-nas, holding forth the truth (hey!) / Buil-ding lives on the word of God / (*falsetto*) Ah-waaah-nuuuh, stands."

Everybody went. Frances figured the cost of me being a double outcast (black and heathen) was more than that of her having to reeducate me in the sanity of our own home on Friday morning. Really, she just didn't understand the awesome power of plastic crap. Plus, I was one of the fifteen kids that went to the exclusively cultish Avalon Christian Academy, where I'd been convinced more than once that yes, I was, in fact, a bastard (no offense, just officially) but also mercifully redeemable. So looking back, it's understandable that one day I would point her attention to Leviticus, chapter 18, verse 20: "You shall not lie with a male as with a woman; it is an abomination."

No one had showed me this particular passage beforehand in an effort to sneakily gauge our wickedness. Frances's status was like the sixth finger that gets yanked off otherwise perfect babies: people see the small but noticeable bump on your pinkie, but no one says, "Hey, you're technically mutated." Everyone knew. Once, before bedtime at my new best friend Melissa's, her mother nailed an addendum onto the Lord's Prayer that Frances would "find a man, oh please Lord." The real miracle was that I succeeded in keeping my head down, looking devout without suffering church giggles. I found Leviticus on my own. I'd been reading the Bible before bedtime, inducing nightmares that involved sulfur, hot pokers, pillars of salt, and/or the violent gouging of eyes. If hell had a mascot, I figured it'd be me—illegitimate aberration that I was. If heaven had an album out, the theme song to *The Cosby Show* would be its title track.

◇◇◇◇◇◇

In the Huxtables I found a family so different from mine. They were huge and permanent. The Andrewses were just two and in constant motion like a tongue. The TV family life looked a lot like how hers did in photo albums. I wanted to be a child like Frances was a child. She had seven brothers and sisters. I had none. She had both father and mother. I had just the one Frances. She'd fallen in love with my dad, Billy, in high school and had his kid ten years later, which was long after she admitted to herself that she loved women.

To hear her tell it, Frances's girlhood was something supernatural. Her stories were stuffed with penny candies, backyard circuses, crossed eyes, fear of canned fish, and matching Easter dresses. I wanted to be her sister, not her daughter. That was impossible, sure, but you get the picture. I wanted picturesque.

Without knowing, she regifted me all of that in Catalina. I stayed out until ten at night because nobody there would steal me. Everyone knew to whom I belonged. We never locked our doors. It was a 1950s sitcom with '90s commercial breaks. When KFC debuted the new barbecue honey wings, we stood in line on Main Street. Yes, Main Street. Because the streets are so small, most people drive around in golf carts. The fancy ones sat four. We had one jail, run by the sheriff, who was also the mayor. Summer Saturdays were spent entirely at the beach. We'd race to a floating platform less than a quarter mile from the shore called "the float," lie on top of it for ten minutes, swim back, and then repeat. When a doctor looked at my pee for a routine checkup, there was sand in it. Tommy, a retired policeman with a buzz cut who still wore his uniform, waited for me by the post office every morning just to say "hi" as I walked to school. He'd make the seaweed green mass that used to be a tattoo of a hula girl dance if I begged. There was one movie theater in the old casino, and it played one movie a week. Frances and I saw *Fried Green Tomatoes* there with an old white guy I think she was on a date with. Afterward she said that Idgie and Ruth were really "lovers." She wanted *everything* to be gay.

My other best friend was a beautiful blonde with brown freckles named Wendy. Full disclosure: she was *my* best friend. I'm not entirely positive I was hers. The sterling-silver-plated "Best Friends" heart necklaces were $16.95 including tax in some plastic crap catalog. What you did was break it along a prefabricated jagged line. One girl wore "st ends," and her soul mate took "Be Fri." Everybody wanted the "Be Fri" half, since it was an unintentional complete sentence. We were big into grammar. And like every other girl in Mrs. Paul's sixth-grade class, I wanted Wendy to wear my "st end." We fought over syntax.

"Well, you can't be 'Be Fri' because you'd be a burned fry," she said in front of everybody who was anybody. I laughed before admitting that she was right. What was I thinking? We never got the necklaces. I worshipped her anyway.

Wendy's house was up a dirt road we called Monkey Hill. With the burned junk food incident behind us, we started hanging out a lot after posters for the annual Rotary Club talent show started showing up around school. Wendy, along with a tall sociopath named Shelly, wanted us to perform "Stop! In the Name of Love." The three of us sang along to a cassette after school and practiced our repetitive hand motions, the self-defense move for "Stop!" and cork-screwing two fingers from head to shoulder for "think it oo-oo-vah." The genius part was that Wendy wanted to wear "foundation," you know, to look more like the Supremes. Awesome idea. I told Frances I needed to borrow some of her makeup. She asked me what for, and I told her. Wrong. *Can you believe these fools wanted to perform in blackface?* She talked to

Wendy's mom. I performed a solo "Wind Beneath My Wings" and won third place. I think people expected me to be good.

The other would-be Supreme, Shelly, was two years older than me and a stalker. She wanted a monogamous thing that I wasn't ready for. I slept over her house once, and Shelly convinced me that girls shouldn't wear underwear to bed. I think she meant bras. Either way, she creeped me out. Immediately I started avoiding her and kept my panties on. She knocked on our door one day and I wrapped myself up in a curtain like a cocoon, or if she decided to murder me that day, a winding sheet. Shelly saw me peeking out to see if she'd bought it. No such luck. I was about to duck back in, but I'd already been spotted. Staring straight at me, her eyes burning, she shouted, "That is so rude!" from our front steps, whipping around on her jellies and trotting back up the hill to her own house. She barely spoke to me the next day at lunch, even when everyone begged to trade after Frances dropped off my Tuesday pizza (we could never get it together at the beginning of the week, so I was "homeschooled" on Mondays and got two slices of pepperoni delivered for lunch on Tuesdays). Knowing I had a weak stomach, Shelly whispered aloud that the oregano was really dried-up boogers. I gave her both slices.

This was also around the time she told me *The Cosby Show* was dumb because it "wasn't really real."

"Oh, please. She's only saying that because it's a doctor and a lawyer and they're both black," explained Frances, slowly cementing my hatred. "Tell her she doesn't have to watch. Nobody's forcing her." Smelly Shelly was an asshole, and Frances, my mother, was a hero.

And so every Thursday night, I'd make the decision to either sing cult classics with the tiny racists of our town or lie on Frances's lap, listening to "the best elevator music I ever heard." It was always my choice. Frances never forced me in either direction.

"I don't feel like Awanas tonight," I'd say while washing dishes, leaving a dirty cast-iron skillet on one side of the sink for her to wash because the deal was I didn't have to do pots.

"Okay, little brown-eyed girl," she'd say, never knowing how guilty I felt.

In the beginning I was good—memorizing verses, earning new patches for the gray vest that "cubbies" wore, holding my praise arms way above my head, my eyes closed to "Lord I Lift Your Name on High." The anointed saw a little black girl saved— eyes shut in a true exercise of faith—but the whole time I was daydreaming of Clair. Of being talented and beautiful and having strong men whose names you knew, whose names you shared. In fact, I wanted to be Rudy, to love Clair, and to be loved by Cliff. Before the opening credits were over, I'd call up Mel, shout, "I'm Rudy!" into the receiver, and hang up before she could object. We spent a lot of time dreaming up all the things we'd do when we became "business women."

That's another big difference between the Huxtables and us: money. My favorite episode was the one where big sister Denise makes younger brother Theo a Gordon Gartrelle knockoff because Cliff won't buy a designer shirt for a fifteen-year-old. Frances wouldn't get me Jordache jeans, and I never understood why not. She had more jobs than fingers: waitressing in white shorts at Antonio's, selling vacation condos at Hamilton Cove, founding the Catalina Youth Arts Exchange, bathing and changing an old lady who'd had a stroke, doing something at Parks and Rec, and starting her own landscaping business called Greenier Pastures (The "ier" was my idea because it stood for the greenest green possible). It was my babysitter who thought it necessary to inform me of our broke-ness, asking one day if I considered myself "high class, middle class, or low class." After thinking for a minute, I hollered "Middle class" while lobbing my arms in a V shape like a cheerleader.

She sucked her teeth. "Really?"

The shirt Denise makes Theo is hideola, of course, but anything looks good after thirty minutes. Between commercial breaks he grows to love it. I'm guessing the message was either "Don't judge a book by its cover" or "Clothes don't make the man." My takeaway was, "Even rich kids have cheap parents." And "Being an only child blows." If I wanted a pair of Jordaches, I'd have to cobble them together from "there's nothing wrong with these" garage-sale finds myself.

My other favorite *Cosby Show* episode was the one when Cliff takes Rudy and her friends to a fancy restaurant, and everybody orders burgers. Frances and I used to have burgers and root beer floats at a regular place in our old Los Angeles life, memories of which were steadily being swallowed whole by seagulls. There's another Rudy-centric episode that was written for me. In it, she's been invited to a birthday party and wants to wear a purple plaid summer dress. It being winter in Brooklyn, Clair's laid out something with long sleeves. There's a fight, and Rudy's sent to her room. Up there by herself, she tries to take her mind off having her life ruined—she does a quick waltz with Bobo the bear (boring), tries to read an oversize book in her rocking chair (no good), and then spots the dress hanging on her closet door (irresistible). Rudy presses it against her chest like an old lover and does one final spin in front of the mirror, probably hoping that things will turn around like magic. But then she remembers how much her life sucks and flings the dress in a trunk, locking it away until next summer. This entire depressing montage is underscored by Kermit the Frog's "It's Not Easy Being Green." Try being brown in a sea of white surrounded by blue.

The real-life person who played Rudy, Keshia Knight Pulliam, was the black Hayley Mills of the early nineties. She starred in a TV movie called *Polly* (Mills's *Pollyanna* remixed). I waited weeks for this television event, even recorded it, making sure to stop the tape during the commercials. Mrs. Paul, my sixth-grade guru, had said I could show it in class that Friday, which was usually reserved for listening to her read. *Roll of Thunder, Hear My Cry* is the only book I remember, which is funny considering how much I hated it. The story was about a black family trying to survive Jim Crow. *Never heard of him.* Once, before it was time for everyone to lay their heads on their desks and get hypnotized by the many voices of Mrs. Paul, she called me up to the front to show me something. I was both honored and horrified.

"Helena, I'm going to point to a word and I want you to tell me what you think about it." She was holding the open paperback in one hand and underlining the word "nigger" with the other. I stared at the page long enough to recognize my own nickname. Immediately the carefully prepared comeback for whenever I heard the word on the playground—"I may be stupid, but I ain't a nigger, ain't a nigger, ain't a nigger . . . ," sung in a robot voice—came to mind.

Without looking up from the page, I said I was fine with it. She said she could gloss over it somehow, but I told her again that I was okay.

"Are you sure?" Mrs. Paul was somewhere between the ages of like forty-one and maybe seventy-three.

"Umm-hmmm." I made an about-face and walked back to my table, no. 12.

"Whud she wan?" asked Bo, whose desk faced mine and whose face I dreamed of at night.

"Nothing."

Polly was my revenge. Not against Mrs. Paul. She was a fantastic. She got breast cancer twice and still smoked in secret when we were at recess. There was a test she gave every year—the "pay attention" quiz. All you had to do to pass was ignore her. It had maybe ten questions, each one more random than the last:

No. 2— Lick your thumb and then smudge it next to the space provided.

No. 4— Switch chairs with the person to your left, wait four and one half seconds, then switch back.

No. 7— Stand on your chair and recite the 5 times table from 2 to 10, skipping every answer ending in 0.

No. 10— Shout out "I'm finished" after playing the piano on your desk. Choose any song you like.

During all this, Mrs. Paul was clucking like a chicken while tap-dancing on top of randomly selected desks, and rule No. 1 said not to laugh, keep your eyes on your paper. What most of us didn't bother to do was read the instructions at the top of the page, which said to write your initials on the back and sit quietly until she called time. Paying attention was worthless if you didn't start out right to begin with.

Polly would be a new beginning for me. The day I brought the tape in, I felt powerful, like when you know a secret that other people don't realize that they should know. I had a G14-classified VHS in my JanSport and was waiting for the perfect moment to slam it down on someone's desk. *Oh, you thought you knew what a black girl was? Well, take. A Look. At this!* Minds would be blown. After two hours, everyone would know what me was: well, me if I was a singing orphan in 1950s Alabama. Whatever. It was a start.

Someone from the AV club rolled in a two-hundred-pound twenty-inch. Mrs. Paul called my name, and I got to walk all the way from table no. 12 to the front of the room to pop in the tape and press play. The whole way back, I couldn't stop smiling. Once we got rolling, even Johnny Leonardi laughed, and I was pretty sure he was plotting to kill me one day, or at least trip me en route to sharpening a pencil. Everybody liked it. They ooooohed when the old white doctor who looked like the Kentucky Colonel calls Polly a "pickaninny," having the faint intuition that it meant something bad (Frances had to explain it to me). We all cheered at the end when Polly cuts the ribbon, christening the newly built bridge that joins the white part of town to the black part.

I thought my life might change after that. I thought I might be invited to more sleepovers with Barbies and less Bible studies. I thought someone might pick me first for something. Anything.

Not so much. But I did score points for getting us out of reading hour, which I'd personally hated since Mrs. Paul read the word "nigger" out loud. Sure, I told her it was fine, but I didn't think she'd actually do it:

Little Man bit his lower lip, and I knew that he was not going to pick up the book. Rapidly, I turned to the inside cover of my own book and saw immediately what had made Little Man so furious. Stamped on the inside cover was a chart which read:

CHRONOLOGICAL ISSUANCE	[. . .] 12
DATE OF ISSUANCE	September 1933
CONDITION OF BOOK	Very Poor
RACE OF STUDENT	nigra

Then the main character goes, "S-see what they called us." Then Mrs. Paul with all her ancient oratory skills goes, (*evil redneck old teacher voice*) "That's what you are" (*normal nonracist voice*) "she said coldly" (*racist voice*) "Now go sit down."

Sixty-six tiny eyeballs stuck to the back of my head for the rest of the hour.

Thankfully, they couldn't actually see in there. Otherwise they'd know the secrets I was too afraid to say out loud, even when I was alone. To my limited knowledge, none of my friends knew that Frances was a gay. I carried around *our* status as lesbians—her by choice, me by association—like a bedazzled scarlet *A*. Someone might notice while Frances helped the normal mothers pass out Rice Krispies Treats or when she bared her unshaven legs at one of my Little League games.

One time, a girl I knew from Awanas, LeAnne, had to go for one week with a King James Bible handcuffed to her arm with tight string. She'd been bad or something. It hung from her wrist ball-and-chain-style for a few days before Frances made her cut it off. LeAnne cried. "If your dad has a problem with it, tell him to call me." Those were the days that I never wished her different.

Then there were the times when I danced with a towel on my head. My other favorite Cosby episodes were any with Cliff and Clair dancing. The lights had been dimmed in their mansion, and both were wearing silk pajamas. Someone would put a record on the player they kept on the desk near the front door in the living room, and jazz would come purring out. The ideal '80s ebony egalitarians. I learned the steps in our one-room apartment with the shared bathroom down the hall.

The cheek to cheek, feet to feet. When I was alone, which was increasingly always, I'd carefully fix a white towel along my hairline and practice. Bath towels were best because they were longer. You could twist them counterclockwise at the nape of your neck and flip the bottom half over your left shoulder, seductively—very Diana Ross in *Mahogany*. Anyway, this is what I did when Wendy and "the girls" were having secret sleepovers they forgot to tell me about on Friday but had no problem remembering the details of by Monday—two-step with a towel on my head and a teddy bear in my arms.

Black romance was my imaginary friend. Our members-only club was me, Rudy, Clair, and Cliff—if we felt like letting boys in that day. Frances, though perfect to me by biology, wasn't allowed.

It didn't matter that this was before her presence at everything—recitals, rehearsals, camps, and competitions—was more embarrassing than endearing. I loved it when she popped up in my school world with a boxed cake or bag of Valentine's candy. *This is my mother, people. See, someone thinks this much of me.* I rarely wished for a father then. Or that she shaved her pits.

But on Thursdays, no matter where I was—surrounded by little lilies of the valley or snuggled into Frances's mommy belly—the oddity of my existence on earth was so acute that I'd get a prickling in my fingers and go into a waking trance I called "the sticks." I never tried to explain "the sticks" to Frances, because I hardly understood them myself, and was certain they'd make me sound nuts. It happened in one of two places: the toilet or the couch. I'd be sitting there minding my own business or taking care of some business, and "the sticks" would come to get me. Time stopped, images would blur Siamese, and then a gazillion invisible little toothpicks would stab at my body while my mind pulled me in as many directions. I could've sat there for hours, contemplating things far beyond my maturity level (even now). Topics A through Z included the meaning of life, why people called me black when I was clearly brown, my grandmother's hatred, the sensation of swallowing spit, sounding out the word *lame*. Then I'd blink, and it'd all be over. Back to pooping or loafing around.

When the theme music for *The Cosby Show* came on, "the sticks" would try to take me over, but I'd force them out through my fingers. I had to pay attention and study this life I planned on living someday. Yeah, I longed for us to be the Huxtables, but I would've settled for living next door to them. I wanted to fit in on that block "over town" somewhere in the life we'd floated away from. No wonder Clair became my secret crush. And because my biological father and I were in a no-titles relationship, I clung to Cliff just as hard. These TV people were real. It was my life on a faraway island that was fake.

When our black-and-white TV went off, I was by myself again.

In the end, I just wanted to make sure she knew that we were most likely going to hell, that she was *aware* of the decision she'd made for the both of us. I was concerned. After convincing myself that she most desperately needed my help, I marched into the living room.

"Have you seen this?" I said, much more softly than originally planned. In my head it was more of a booming accusation, but in real life it came out like a question, cowering over in the corner somewhere.

I did manage to shove my open King James onto her lap. Too scared to actually read the text aloud, despite being an excellent out-loud reader, I pointed to the page and waited.

She said Grandmommy had shown her that same page years ago. She never said the word *gay*, *lesbian*, *vagina*, *homo*, or *dyke*. There was no script, no prepared lines. I was perfectly normal, she said, and so was she. She didn't say anything about us going to hell or heaven, though. I figured we were there already.

RIDING IN CARS
WITH LESBIANS

Epiphanies over Ethiopian are probably worth the indigestion.
When it occurred to me—with a mouth too full of *injera* to
object—that Britanya knew me better than I knew myself and
also wanted to *know* me in the biblical sense, I did what any self-
hiding heterosexual woman would: practiced willful ignorance
until the problem went away and life returned to nonchalance.

"You're just so . . . robotic," observed Britanya, disrupting the
funnels of smoke shooting out her nose as if it were an exhaust
pipe. Totally disgusting. Kind of sexy.

"Pffft! What the hell are you talking about?" It had to be the
spicy lamb stuff that was making me sweat. Or possibly the
cancer fumes. This chick didn't even know me like that. Give or
take, we'd shared six bitch sessions in the copy room, five non–
work-related phone calls, four field trips to U Street, three blind

dates with dudes, two sex talks, and one sleepover. And all that was after I found out she was a little bit lesbian via some innocent MySpace snooping induced by work boredom. There was a blog post on "Writer Chick's" page about how she'd been heartbroken by a "her." Current mood? Sad face.

Clearly I was next on her hit list. "Umm, she wants your body, dude," Gina agreed. In spite of or because of this, I let Britanya pick the restaurant.

"I mean," she started in her best I've-looked-at-another-woman's-vag'-up-close-and-saw-the-meaning-of-life voice, "you talk about all this shit that obviously affected you like it didn't affect you, like it's nothing." Now she was gesticulating—you know, that thing people do to supersize their emotion, when they make their hands like cups, hunch their backs over, and push the air in front of their heart in your direction. It's like they're offering it to you or something. Whatever, it's weird and hard to explain, but that's what she was doing, and that's what was freaking me out. Because this could only mean one of two things: (1) she was having a bad reaction to the *wot*, or (2) she'd gotten me so down pat that in her mind only heavy petting could follow.

◇◇◇◇◇

We were the black ones, both working as Hebrew slaves in the Washington bureau of the *New York Times*. All during my interview I was made to feel more comfortable by the consistently random mentioning of her first name. "You should probably get Britanya's take on Washington . . . ," and "Britanya went to college too . . . ," and "Come to think of it, Britanya also breathes oxygen. . . ." I sweah foh Gawd somebody was about to yell, *See! We've got another one! And her name's super black!* When we did finally meet, I was disappointed, suddenly realizing that I was just as big of a name-racist as everyone else. Bree-TEHN-yuh was a sorority girl with a southern accent and a love for the spoken word, not some high school dropout who, through a series of ups and downs and the help of Oprah's Angel Network, finally made good.

She was one of those people who denounce Facebook for being so "high school," but then decide to announce a hiatus from said juvenile distraction in a blog, then a status update, an away message, and finally a mass e-mail. So despite her being anti-everything, it didn't take much digging to find out Britanya lived for a year with a woman that was more than a roommate. By now, though, she was into men, specifically this one dude named Rasheed, Raj for short, who she said wrote MySpace blogs that spoke to her. Introducing a virus to their computer love was a girl named Kim, aka Ms. Apple Bottom Baltimore (seriously), who wanted an "experience" with Britanya. They'd "made out" once, Britanya dumped her, and then Kim friended Raj on MySpace, which, of course, induced a titty attack in Britanya that only subsided after she kicked Raj out of her apartment the morning after they did it for the first time. She told me she loved him. The whole thing lasted like two months.

Despite her occasional penchant for the p-word, I figured she knew I didn't get down like that, and if I did, it wouldn't be with someone who wore peasant skirts in 2006. I could've been her straight wife if she hadn't been so smoky, drunk, and right that night at Dukem's Fine Ethiopian Cuisine.

"I'm just saying," Britanya said again. "You talk and talk and talk and talk about all this heavy shit that I know affected you in some kind of way like the shit doesn't matter. It does. You *have* feelings."

I fell silent and then did what came naturally to me: totally removed myself from the situation, like how they do in gangs.

Gave her a few umm-hmms, paid half the bill, walked her to the metro, and never spoke to her again.

There was only one other time when my voice got lost on its way somewhere important. I was newly pubescent and tired of hearing shushed arguments from my mom and her current "mate" Vernell's bedroom. To remedy this, I wrote fake Chinese, or maybe they were forgotten hieroglyphics, on a refrigerator dry-erase board every day until they got so creeped out the three of us had a "talk" about all the things I wanted to say but couldn't. This made sense to them. "Fine" became my secret "Fuck you." They left after an hour of assurances, feeling good about their parenting skills and my apparent sanity.

Then the blood day happened, I turned thirteen, and my voice changed.

We were back living in Los Angeles, and I was on scholarship at a prep school. Vernell would pick me up most days. Without my having to ask, she never got out of the car. In order to avoid any "my mom's here" confusion—seeing as how I had two—by 3:20 p.m., I'd already staked out a spot on the outside lunch table nearest the pickup zone, on the lookout for a gray '92 Nissan. Already at the gate by the time she came to a rolling stop, I'd run to the car, yank open the door, and dive in the front passenger's seat like a bank robber with a bad feeling about this. "Drive!" I wanted to shout, taking a triumphant glance backward at the dust-covered cops we'd left behind. Instead, I leaned the seat back as far as it could go and told her about my day.

Every story involved the Nubian Sisters, the eighth-grade black girls club in which I had the most peripheral of memberships. Gina had full privileges, while I mainly stood on the sidelines, lying about getting my period and getting tongue. The real oral exam was knowing all the words to Too $hort's "I'm a Player." I listened to 92.3 The Beat with blind people ears until I was ready to whisper the lyrics in the hallway when teachers weren't around. "See, I made up my mind when I was seventeen. I ain't wit no marriage and weddin' ring. I be a playa fo' life." The clique's unofficial bard, a girl named Monique, changed up some of the lyrics to fit our current circumstances. Instead of "I used to fuck young ass hoes / I used to be broke and didn't have no clothes," we sang, "I used to get the young ass sperm / Used to be broke and had a messed-up perm." Just turned thirteen, and already jaded.

Our real anthem ushered in the opening credits of *Living Single*, a new show starring Queen Latifah as a man-loving magazine editor. Really, it was our fight song—"Ooooo, in a '90s kinda woo-oorld I'm glad I've got my girls!" At the time, this didn't seem depressing.

Living Single was the new reality we little brown-eyed girls had to look forward to. A bunch of grown-ass women living together—in fucking Brooklyn. Monique dubbed herself Regine, the calculating fashion vixen. Gina was Khadijah, the sporty career woman. Marissa was Max, the man-eating lawyer. They said I could be Synclaire, the ditzy virgin. Pretty much everyone was having some version of sex but me—on screen and in life. I still thought I was more like Max—smart, driven, and possibly gay since, you know, she was so smart and driven. Plus, she had short hair—extra gay.

On the way home, Vernell and I would listen to The Beat's promos for the show, which was new and '90s. She loved this one line they played on repeat. It was Max talking about what women should do with men—"Snip. Snip." To drive the point home she scissored the air in front of my eyes with her fingers. A would-be peace sign turned into a scalpel.

Vernell was the one who taught me how to use a tampon in our bathroom before I needed to learn. Said it was important to know, "just in case." She was the one who told me that I should probably try sex before I got married, because "you never know." She was the one who convinced me to wear gigantor neon green Cross Colours. Said it looked cool. She was the one from New York. We moved to Los Angeles two years after the riots to be close to her. Almost ten years younger than Frances, she was the one I thought knew everything.

Spending quality time in the Nissan with Vernell also meant time spent listening to her criticize my mother for not raising me right or me for being such a snob.

"So now that you go to a new school, you're too good to hang out with Shonda?" There was contention in her voice. Shonda, the long-legged girl who lived across the street, liked to five-finger troll dolls and let boys do the same to her. After I got into Pilgrim, *she* was the one who thought she was too cool for my school. I was the one in a pleated plaid skirt with no one to talk to. Vernell knew none of this.

I sat on my side of the car in silence.

"Your mother is not a people person," she explained as we rolled over Olympic Boulevard, watching the magical palm trees of Beverly Hills turn into mangy ones. A poor man's palm tree is just as tall but lacks the grace. Instead of swaying, the palm trees on our block slumped, the branches made heavy by dirt, not fluttering with fairy dust. "I can get along with just about anybody, but not your mom. Oh, no, not Frances. She doesn't know how to talk to people, you know?"

Having not yet learned the definition of *rhetorical*, I saw my continued silence as cowardice. Vernell was first on my Chinese hit list.

A .99 Cent Store dry-erase board saved my life. I'd never given the thing much thought before using it to slash manic slaps of marker onto our Frigidaire. Prior to it becoming the major outlet of my innermost angst, the three of us used it for grocery lists and homework reminders. Some girls cut, chuck, or fuck. I transcribed.

The grown-ups were in the living room arguing during the commercials, trading insults to a sound track about sunglasses. Frances, we need to talk about this. *My name is Geek I put 'em on as a shocker.* Do whatever you want, Vernell, leave me out of it. *Man, I love these Blublockers.* I hate you. *Everything is clear.* Keep your voice down. *They block out the sun.* Why? Helena knows what a bitch you are. *Oh yeah, I gotta get me some.*

Escaping the dissonance meant walking through the kitchen and past the shiny plastic slab that would become my Rosetta stone.

At first it looked like fine art, all impressionist and stuff. Mimicking the moves of a painter like how people do when they conduct pretend orchestras, I used the marker like a brush, flicking quick and dirty strokes on the message board in neat Koranic lines. Subconscious calligraphy. It looked Arabic, alien, oriental, hieroglyphic. My hand was possessed. Ignorant of whatever it was I was writing, I just "wrote."

One night, after a particularly edifying ride in the Nissan (seems Vernell wanted a baby—the old-fashioned way, with the penis and the sex and etc.), I tried to get Frances to go to her, comfort her, shut her up, with an especially pleading "Mom . . ." She actually said it was "grown folks' business"—and I was shut down by a cliché.

Then the dry-erase board started doing the talking for me. Each bundle of madness represented a tiny character in my pretend alphabet. The scene was bloody, all thick black ink and serial killer-y. When it was over, I snapped the cap back on my new weapon and admired the damage I'd done. *Just wait until they see this shit.* When I was done I felt normal again, righted. I practiced my daily hieroglyphics for weeks, figuring madness on my part might preclude a melee on theirs. It did not.

Screams are as scarce as the monsters they allegedly shield us from. Barring East European Michael Jackson extremists, nobody screams in everyday life. It's not something that's done outside of amphitheaters and horror films. So when one hears an earsplitting screech not too far in the distance, it's a singular moment. A moment that marks you for good, like a leftover fake Chinese character on a dry-erase board.

"Well, at least I'm not raising a daughter with no feelings!" I heard Vernell shriek, placing as much emphasis on the word *feelings* as one can when speaking in Soprano. I was sitting on the edge of my bed, too scared to go to the door but brave enough not to take this lying down. It was an insult, obviously, but I was far from offended.

I had plenty of fucking emotions. I just keep 'em between me and the fridge.

"Don't you dare talk about my daughter," Frances growled in a register so low I thought at first she might be joking. Like they were rehearsing lines or something for *The Exorcist meets Freddy*. It sounded like my mother was talking not through her teeth but against them, trying to grind them down or shatter them with her snarling. I figured she didn't need my help.

Then there was the drum roll of so many dictionaries falling to the floor, and that sound gradually evolved into the rumbling of an earthquake, and a crack like thunder, and then a sort of silence. Digging my fingers into my comforter, I strained to hear something comforting, something familiar like more yelling, more insults, more "fuck this." Nothing. The dangerous kind of quiet.

They were rolling around the living room in their panties when I ran in, punching each other in the back and scratching at each other's arms, I think. All I could see was a revolving brown ball of lesbian. Two women trying desperately to shove the truth into the other through any means necessary. How or why they were half naked I don't know. The whole scene would have seemed smutty to an equally naked eye if it weren't so ridiculous. Two grown women, on the wrong side of thirty-five and 205 pounds, wrestling like professional amateurs. I didn't know what to do besides watch.

Vernell stood up and started beating my mother from above, pushing her fists into her shoulders and the top of her head. Frances, who'd I'd never seen so weak, was shielding her head and surrendering simultaneously.

"Go ahead, beat me. Beat me," she was whimpering in a voice I'd never heard and never wanted to hear again. Vernell obliged, and Frances sank even lower to the floor. She had no neck, no shoulders, no head, and no arms. The woman who was once so much bigger than me didn't just become smaller in my eyes; she practically disappeared, leaving a puppy or some other defenseless thing in her place.

"Don't you. Hit. My mother," I managed to force out with a voice half high-pitched and half baritone. I didn't plan to say that. I had planned on just screaming or something, maybe throwing a glass against the wall to get them both to stop and realize how very foolish they looked. But I never planned to defend. I also never called Frances "mother" unless my friends were around. Formality seemed necessary.

I repeated it. Louder this time.

"DON'T YOU DARE HIT MY MOTHER!" I stepped into the ring they'd built—scattered couch cushions and broken picture frames were the ropes—and karate-chopped the air between them. Hopefully cutting off any loose ends. I hadn't meant for it to come out *that* ballsy. She was still my sort-of stepmother. But

I was serious, and I'd surprised all three of us. Vernell, already standing, backed herself into the wall behind us and put her hands to her face, either to check to see if she was bleeding or to see if she was, in fact, all there. If this was really happening.

Pulling my mother from the floor, I put one arm over her shoulder and used the other hand to grip her powerless bicep. Not sure if I was doing it right, I led her naked, limp body to the bathroom, crossing the kitchen and my dry-erase board on the way. Vernell followed us, spitting on my mother's back before I slammed the door in her face. So far being a teenager sucked.

I sat Frances on the toilet like you'd do a child in training and thought of her tin can.

When I was a little kid, I discovered my mother's secrets under her bed, sealed away in a large canister-type thing decorated with nude pictures of women wearing 1970s Afros. In it were love letters she'd written to white girls and journals I think she was writing to me. She talked about "having good romps" with a lady in Argentina and dreams she'd had of a child named "Hellenea."

I found letters from my father in there. They were the only things I had of his, and I imagined the sound of his voice reading them aloud, like in the movies. In my head it was throaty and scratchy—a real man's. In one he said he loved and missed her. In another he said he hoped she hadn't been "taking too many showers with white girls." After that, I knew she was more than just wonderfully different. She was "gay." An invisible man delivered one of the most important headlines of my life.

Well, not entirely invisible. There was a picture of him in there too. He wore a black 'fro, flip-flops, and a sailor's uniform. He had long legs and light skin. This was him.

I imagined he was on the moon, and if I hoped for him enough, thought of him enough, prayed for him enough, he'd come back down. I didn't need saving, but I needed something. Every night for years I repeated the same line to baby Jesus or grown-up Jesus—whomever was listening: "Dear Lord, please let our paths cross someday." We didn't even have to talk or even know who the other one was. I just wanted him to see me.

If he could see us in the bathroom—Frances on the toilet wiping up angry tears, and me running hot water over a washcloth—he'd have to be proud.

There was blood on her back. Not in copious amounts or anything 911-worthy, but there was blood. Enough to usher me into puberty without any cramps of my own. Regardless of what I'd told the Nubes at school, I hadn't gotten my period yet, but this, my official blood day, would do. I dabbed it away while she sat alone on the toilet. This used to be the best seat in the house, from which I watched Vernell pluck her eyebrows, apply her lipstick, and correctly insert a tampon. That day it became the headquarters of my adulthood.

◇◇◇◇◇◇

See, I know a little something about lovers' quarrels and feelings and a whole bunch of other shit. Heavy shit? Yes, my shit is, in fact, heavy. But it's mine! Britanya, Miss "I've put my tongue in places the sun don't shine," couldn't have it, didn't deserve it, and wouldn't be able to wash it down with her *awaze tibs*.

According to my view of the world, the two of us had an appropriate work-friend/actual-friend balance. The only other time we'd hung out for real for real was at the row house next door to mine. I was cool with my neighbors, who liked foreign wine and African drums. Britanya came with. We got super drunk and stumbled back to my bat cave. It was late and the trains had already stopped running. Britanya would have to sleep in a faded

"CU Cheer" T-shirt on a mattress of pillows in my bedroom. She could have just slept on the couch, but she didn't.

In the morning I tiptoed out to the bathroom, careful not to step on her head. I didn't make her breakfast or anything. She didn't say she'd call me. But it was obvious things had changed. We were now work best friends with an infinitesimal dash of sexual tension. With that came the foreseeable bout of verbal diarrhea that wearers of peasant skirts inevitably suffer from. She got comfortable. Then we got Ethiopian.

Obviously I wasn't going to respond in kind. Telling intimate details about my private life to a work wife I was trying to separate from? Um, no. So as to whet her appetite but not her lady parts, I told her that my mom was a lesbian, that my grandmother kidnapped me when I was a kid in order to save us from a life of Spanish crack whoredom, that Frances had been in a crazy abusive relationship when I was in middle school but that we got out of it by escaping to my dead grandfather's house in Compton, and that I commuted two hours a day from there to get to a private school downtown, where I was a super genius who eventually got into the Ivy League, therefore setting in motion my evil plot to set the world ablaze.

"You're just so robotic," Britanya said.

"What do you even mean by that? You hardly know me."

"You say stuff like it's nothing. Like you don't even care." She sounded concerned, but also curious.

"Well, I don't know what to tell you." I was being honest.

Then we split the bill, and I walked her to the metro station. The next day I translated our heart-to-heart into IM chatter—"then she's all ure so robotic . . . gtfoh." "Dude, she just wants your body. She doesn't even know you like that. Ignore." And I did.

MILEAGE

My dog, Miles, is super racist.

He's a self-loathing six-month-old black pug that routinely goes ape-shit whenever the Corner Negroes from our neighborhood come anywhere near his miniature personal space. I found him out just days after deciding to "get a puppy rather than a baby," in my mother's humble opinion.

It happened when we were walking together—Miles and me—for the first time on W Street over by the Flagler Market, a quaint little "corner store" half a block away from my "luxury" apartment building, which is in the heart of what a friend said used to be "the biggest Jamaican open-air drug market in the mid-Atlantic." Nowadays there's a bunch of street signs that publicize the neighborhood as a "Drug Free Zone," which obviously means it's safe for dogs of the non-pit-bull variety. The day before our introductory stroll around the block, I went into Borders to read and reshelve all the books on pets, puppies, pugs, dogs, dog shows, and dog training. According to the experts, "socialization" is vital; it's everything. The only book I bought, *Pug: A Comprehensive Guide to Owning and Caring for Your Dog*, said, "Lack of socialization can manifest in fear and aggression as the dog grows up. Walk him around the neighborhood, take him on your daily errands, let people pet him. . . ." Fine, then. Off to the market we go.

Now the Flagler Market is a bootleg bodega run by Ethiopians who I'm sure don't call it a bodega in Ethiopian language, but who are running one just the same. The windows are bulletproof and the chicks behind the register refuse to bag anything for you. Instead, they shove something black and plastic through a spinning slot in the indoor drive-thru window; you then shove your dollars in its place and pack that dented can of green beans yourself. One time, I saw a girl with half her hair braided and the other half not, wearing half her ass in cut-off jorts—the other half not. She was there to pick up a "deuce deuce" of St. Ides. The blue kind. I felt nostalgic for freshman year but also deeply saddened for my people. In front of her in line was a house painter (lacking solid evidence of what he actually did for a living, I assumed the overalls slashed in white paint were occupational). He was asking the twins behind the prison pane for a "nutrition bar." They were still busy pointing at cigarettes and Snickers when he left.

The dregs of LeDroit Park hang around the busted-up concrete slabs that make for a sidewalk outside. I won't assume these men push "product" for a living, but, well, they wear puffy black coats in the summertime. So already they've got on the uniform of a corner-to-corner salesman. A smarter woman—one who wouldn't pay $1,850 a month to live next to a halfway house—would have known that a puppy suspicious of everything save his own balls would feel *uncomfortable* around what Gina calls "the element." Silly me.

Okay, so we're walking. Me and Miles. Him looking doggy fabulous in a red leather collar and "lead" I bought off the Internet for seventy bucks, and me in skinny jeans and knee boots. It's eight in the morning.

Everything's going as laid out in the books—the dog is investigating various blades of grass and vacant bags of Chili Fritos while I hold his leash as if it were a remote control, like how they do on the dog shows—when a Flagler customer (who shops on the corner, not *in* the corner store) comes shuffling out of the alley to our right, dragging his feet as if treading on top of wet cement and clutching the neck of a half-drunk bottle. I give him the same head-nod I give every black man from around the way. It says two things: (1) I see you, and (2) I'm not afraid because we are all one people—and also, I'm one person with pepper spray.

"Oh, that's a pretty little shiny dog you got," he says without slurring, and coming increasingly closer to an increasingly frantic Miles with each compliment. By "dog" he's about three feet away with an open palm, dirt in every crease, but friendly.

Miles does not give a shit about friendly.

"Thank you. He's a little shy, though," I say by way of explaining the poltergeist currently in possession of my dog's body. Miles is having a grand mal seizure. Mr. Flagler, not giving a shit about this, continues on his path of destruction. I'm trying to be an authoritative pack leader (the books said!) by keeping the lead taut even though every muscle in this dog's neck is against me. His eyes are darting from side to side so fast that he might give himself vertigo, which along with the bill for the bald spot on his head is going to cost me. Now he's leaping into the air in an attempt to escape on the wind. Not working. I try dragging him, but he's hit the emergency brake with his front legs stretched out in what looks like a yoga move someone would pay good money to learn. We're parked. Next comes a wiggling technique he must've learned in his former life as a luchador I mentally name the Utter Mileage. *Be the pack leader. Beeee the pack leader.*

"Don't worry, he's not gonna get outta that thing," observes Mr. Flagler, still determined.

Then it happens. The Utter Mileage works his neck in such a way that his collar just gives up out of admiration. Then he darts into the street faster than these three-inch heels can go, never looking back at what he was running from—a stunned junkie, someone out of 650 bucks. Fuck! Note to self: only walk dog in flats from now on. Note to self: buy flats. "Miles! Come on, baby. Come back. Miles-sies? Mi-iles? Sweetie. Come backsies!"

It's Mr. Flagler who tells me to stop chasing him. Let him come to me.

"Just stand still."

"But he's in the effing street!" I yell, wearing the inches down on my boots pacing the sidewalk.

"It's no cars out here. Just stand still and call him. He'll come."

First off, I'm considering the advice of a crack addict who on most days I'd pretend did not exist. If I were religious, which I am not, Mr. Flagler would be my savior-equivalent. Because this whole thing reminded me of that story about Jesus being a smelly bum nobody wanted around until some guy gives him a bath and then Homeless Jesus grants him three wishes via a dead gorilla's hand or whatever. If I were in possession of said magical monkey paw, I'd wish for Miles not to die today. *Just stand still and he'll come.* Pffft! Who are we talking about here? My dog or that elusive *he* I've been waiting for, for like ever? Standing still unfortunately isn't in the black-girl guidebook. So instead I tiptoe across the street, making sure to walk on the balls of my feet so as not to aggravate Miles with the clicking sound of taps on concrete, and seize him by the bonus skin of his neck before he can make another run for it. His body is flopping about like a dead fish, but thankfully he is neither. Mr. Flagler, prophet you are not.

Every hair on Miles's back has rigor-mortised along with the rest of him. He's too traumatized to walk, so I carry him back home sort of cradled in my arms, his legs sticking straight into the air like an upturned tchotchke. If it weren't for all the heavy panting, his hot breath smelling well past its sell-by date, I'd assume him scared to death.

The point is, since the episode with Mr. Flagler (nee Homeless Jesus), Miles and black men just don't mix. He'll sniff a pair of Timbs maybe, but as soon as one of those construction boots-cum–emblem of ghetto masculinity take one step in his direction, he'll turn tail and run behind my legs faster than you can say *socially awwwk-ward*. I was embarrassed at first—the dog I'd named after a jazz legend would lick a hand, any hand, as long as it didn't have pigment on the flip side. He was making me look bad. The white guy up the street who wore all-weather Crocs? Miles loved him. The boys down the block in down jackets? Hated them. His black-man allergies got so bad I started crossing the street whenever a pack of them appeared on the horizon, and they in turn eyed me with sellout suspicion. *It's not me, I swear! My mom grew up Compton. Compton!* "Ay," one would point out excitedly, backhanding the shoulder of another. "That's that dog from *Men in Black!*" I'd smile stupidly and offer a jumpy "ha ha" while safely on the opposite side of the street. Of life.

Even more important than Miles's discriminatory licking practices was the issue of finding a mate—for me. This would be problematic—me happening to like black men very much, and Miles, not so much. But then again, me and men haven't been mixing so well lately either.

"Well, dude, it's not like you got any at the house," said Gina when I told her about what an asshole Miles was.

But she was wrong, for once. Actually, I'd had more than a few. Purchasing another living being, I found out, is a great conversation piece. People want to know his life—weight, height, likes, dislikes, sleeping habits, pooping patterns: *If a tree fell on Miles in the forest, would you hear him?* I figured letting folks come over to see for themselves was the proper thing to do. The book said to socialize him, so I did—lots, and with varying degrees of success.

First there was Cleveland Keith, who liked to answer questions nobody'd asked. For example, we'll be driving in silence— everybody's minding their own business—and then out of nowhere he'll go, "Yeah, so work was good today. . . ." or "Right, yep, the drive down to Atlanta wasn't bad, wasn't bad at all." Umm, for one, no one asked you how work was, and for two, no one cares how your trip went, and for three, shut it! Plus, he always called me "cutie" and pronounced my Christian name all wrong. Coming from him it was very grassroots, very Uh-lei-nah.

Way before I even got Miles, I'd tried to cut Cleveland Keith off—changed my number, moved apartments, and never answered his e-mails with more than two sentences. Probably shouldn't've answered them at all. Genius. Also, he didn't know what sushi was, which didn't stop him from buying me restaurant roses on my birthday. Made me feel like an ungrateful tramp who preferred loose change to a ham sandwich, but that didn't stop me from sending all his calls straight to voice mail. Watching another *Whose Wedding Is It Anyway?* marathon seemed more promising and surprisingly nonpathetic than another phone conversation about his flag football team. Tired of scrolling through my contacts list, imagining all the calls I didn't feel like making, I broke down one horny night and pressed send when his name got highlighted.

"I got a dog," I said with more pep than planned, nudging a sleeping Miles in the butt with my big toe. Not amused. Cleveland Keith would be right over. I figured meeting him outside on the lawn with a drowsy dog would nonverbally suggest two things: (1) I don't really want you in my house, and (2) this visit will be noncommittal.

Post-sexicles (whatever), I told Cleveland Keith that I wasn't ready for a relationship. He should find a nice girl, I said. A good girl. Someone who'd appreciate his being ordinary and not resent him for it. Someone who didn't love Japanese food. But instead of yanking his cuffed jeans back on and storming out in a "whatever, bitch" huff, he spooned the shit out of me, trapping my arms down to my sides and threatening my neck with his lips. Who sleeps like that? The next morning I gave Miles his second bath in as many days, yelling good-bye to Cleveland Keith through the closed bathroom door. After he left, I got a text: "It was good seeing you again, cutie ☺."

Speaking of texts, Tall Thomas has a problem. Another "contact" I normally try to avoid, instead of calling he sends messages, which wouldn't be so annoying if they weren't so annoying. Thom in text:

(10/25 10:36 p.m.):	Helena, u out 2nite, there's sposed 2 b sumthin @ Posh
(10/25 10:50 p.m.):	Yea, I'm on U Street with some folks. Karaoke! Come thru
(10/25 11:31 p.m.):	How long u gon b owt.
(10/25 11:55 p.m.):	I dunno call me.
(10/25 11:56 p.m.):	How much is it? Fun? Who's there?

(10/26 12:45 a.m.):   OMG. You don't know them. Either come or
                          not. Jesus.

(10/26 1:00 a.m.):   Okay so Jesus is there, who else?

If it weren't for unlimited texts, the whole thing would fall
apart. I mean, he's six-foot-forever, lives three blocks away, and
is especially prompt. After I told Tall Thomas about Miles during
an unnecessarily long Gmail convo, his name started popping up
in my "available friends" like a banner ad for hemorrhoid cream
that suspiciously shows up above your inbox right after you've e-
mailed somebody about "up the butt" and "puffy eyes." Google—
God spelled in wingding—had spoken.

We walked the dog around the block together one night—
very couple-y and so not my idea. Miles chose ignorance as a
means of coping. Never acknowledging Thom's existence, he
kept crashing into his ankles and peeing even closer. The next
morning, Thom sent me an e-mail, the body of which consisted
solely of a giant pug's face grooving in front of a psychedelic
backdrop of primary colors spinning like a beach ball. This was
probably supposed to be funny on drugs. "Are you sure you want
to delete this message?" Yes, please.

I was this close to writing Miles into my will when I met a
new guy, Cooper, in New York at a Columbia alumni thingy. So
he'd been fully vetted. He also had an Elizabethan (or maybe
Jacobian?) notch in his chin. Very civilized. An Iraq War vet getting his master's in international spy stuff. I found the link to a
"Veterans for Obama" ad he was in and immediately started debating how loud my fake yelp should be at the end of our
Marine Corps wedding, you know, after we'd walked down the
aisle under a canopy of swords and the last guy takes his, slaps
me on the ass with it, and says, "Welcome to the Marines, Mrs.
_____." So, when Cooper wanted to come for a visit I was . . .

rehearsed. But who knew what the dog might do. Okay, fine, who knew what I might do. Probably jump him too early and then get bored of him. Gina's opinion? "It's 2008, dude." He would come down Friday morning and leave Saturday. Cool, see you then. Dial tone. Wait, what? Does he think he's staying here?

"Dude, where the hell else would he be staying?" Gina was all for it.

"But then he'll be all in my house and stuff. Looking at things and *touching* things," I whined.

"I can't deal with you right now." Despite having no patience for me that day, Gina still approved the following phone script, you know, like how the telemarketers have:

ME (*uncharacteristically nervous*): So it's supposed to be really nice on Friday.

COOPER (*totally unaware*): Yeah, I'm really looking forward to it.

ME: So where do you usually stay when you come down to D.C.?

COOPER: Hmmmm.

I told anybody who'd listen that I didn't want him in my house in order to (1) convince these people that I was virtuous on occasion and (2) make sure I couldn't backslide at the risk of being a humping hypocrite. Visiting me, sure. But being all up in my stuff, seeing all my secret single things—like how I tend to watch TV in a towel straight from the dryer with my hair in a topknot while going to work on my heels with the incredible PedEgg. But it *was* 2008. And he hadn't called in forever. Convinced that an almost-relationship with a live-action G.I. Joe had been blown as a result of me being too non-whorey, for once, for two whole days I settled into a life lived vicariously through the We Channel. So when he did finally call, slipping in the possibility of invading my personal space, my resolve was greatly diluted.

"Sooooo, lemme ask you a question?"

"Shoot!"

"Is it cool if I just crash on your couch, you know, as long as I promise to behave myself?"

Crap. I mean, he'd been to Iraq. Saying no would've been un-American, and since I had no clue where my voter registration stuff was, this might be my one shot at patriotism this year. Now I had to clean my floors, change my sheets, and buy some Bikini Zone.

Coulda saved myself ten bucks because behave himself he did—to the ten-zillionth power. First off, he showed up in his kickables—Timbaland boots and baggy sweats. I'm sorry, aren't you in grad school? Like, is there some reason you're dressed for an Ivy League shootout? Then he had this ginormous duffel bag, which could only have housed one of two things: wardrobe changes well over the heterosexual limit or *all the tools better to kill you with, my dear.* And he was so much skinnier than the guy I eyed from the bar a few weeks earlier. Guess the cocktail adds ten pounds. And as predicted, he's all . . . looking at my stuff—fingering my books and dropping his rucksack on my fancy "just for show" entryway bench. Also, his head was reminiscent of a Nerf ball and his phalanges were very Ancient Chinese Emperor-y. I was sufficiently creeped.

Miles, already not a fan of the black man, especially ones wearing Timbs, was actually wagging his tail. Perhaps he was giving this guy the shake of approval or waving himself into surrender, or maybe he just wanted to take a dump. Either way, I was intrigued. (This dog was steadily becoming the gatekeeper to whatever love life I hoped to have. And if socializing was the key to his happiness, it was becoming the bane of mine. Using him as an excuse to meet up with men was one thing, a normal thing, but using him to excuse myself from uncomfortable meetings was another.) Anyway, Miles's tail is going a mile a minute when Cooper, eager to impress me and my spawnal equivalent, reaches down to execute some kind of petting slash poking slash prodding move that succeeds only in pissing Miles off. He twists his head back to meet his butt and snaps at Cooper like a plastic board-game hippo. Then this six-foot war hero yanks his freakishly long fingers up to his chest so fast you woulda thought my dog was the Taliban—toy division. What man yanks? There is no masculine conjugation of the verb *yank*. Remember that scene in *Pretty Woman* when Julia Roberts the Prostitute yanks her hand from the jewelry box right when Richard Gere the John claps it shut on her white-gloved hand, then she starts laughing like a maniac and everyone feels all fuzzy about sexual exploitation? It was like that.

"Yeah, you know he can't hurt you, right?"

"Ha . . . ha . . . yeah," Cooper says, hiding his fingers underneath his now-pervy-looking chin. Then, in an attempt to preserve his honor, he picks up Miles's leash off the floor as if it were his face. I tell him it's okay, I'll handle it from here.

At this point, we're about five minutes in. The remaining nineteen hours, excruciating in the details, are easiest to catalog in list form:

1. After making it clear that we could eat anything I wanted and then summarily shooting down every "ethnic food" suggestion, including Italian, which so doesn't count, he decided he'd like "American contemporary."

2. When dinner was over, he sincerely asked, "Did you get enough to eat?"

3. His PJs, which he changed into at 11:00 p.m., consisted of waist-high black military-issue shorts that hit above the knee, a tucked-in military-issue T-shirt, and white ankle socks.

4. A tucked. In. T-shirt.

5. White people lips.

6. After smashing his face into mine in what I can only assume was a kiss, he prodded my left boob like an oncologist and then did the same to my left lip. The one your gyno deals with, not your dentist.

7. His Facebook status: "Cooper is wondering if there will be a Midwestern Whitehouse–Obama–Axelrod–Emanuel?"

8. Inappropriate singing of Aaliyah's "Are You That Somebody."

9. Incongruous usage of the interjection "Yo."

10. First thing in the morning, after a long night spent listening to his future CNN sound bites, he said "historic quantity" three times before putting a period on it.

I could go on, but there's no point in further proving what a picky bitch I am. The evidence against me is overwhelming—insurmountable even. Blame it on the dog. No, seriously. See, Miles's unwavering adoration is both unnerving and wholly necessary. He's never more than three doggy steps behind, tracking my every move like a midget voyeur. Making the tiny insignificances of my life momentous. He watches me pee with the intensity of a peeping Tom. If I ever kick him out, he waits outside the bathroom door until I'm done, putting his life on hold for my bowel movements. When I get out of the shower, Miles helps dry my calves with his tongue, then waits patiently to see what lotion I'll choose. Closing my door to go to bed is the apocalypse. My waking up is like the second coming. And I think I deserve all of it, therefore making Cooper's stubborn imperfection all the more unacceptable.

It was like I liked not liking Cooper, or couldn't like him because my emotional reciprocity quotient had been reached via this dog. I got high off the hateration, running through the afore-mentioned list with anyone who asked, which was everyone, since everybody knew he spent the night in my stuff—well, not *in* my stuff, but you get the picture. All the next day I answered the phone, "Lemme tell you how this cat . . ." But before I could start bitching, I had to get him to leave.

As soon as Cooper's eyes pop open, his mouth does the same. He wants to discuss the "historical quantity" of Barack Obama's presidency some more and then maybe play Guess Who? with his cabinet picks. This has got to be some kind of combat technique—talking me into surrender or possibly another mammogram. No, thank you, sir, I don't want another!

"Yeah, weren't you getting up?" I say from my new side of the bed while Cooper lies on my other side.

"Yep, yep. Gotta hit the road and see my old commander . . ." Before he could finish, there was a scratch at the door, then a sniff, and then a scratch, and then a sniff, and then a . . .

Inhaling the shadowy line of space under the bedroom door,

clawing at its frame like a junkie jonesing for his next Helena fix, Miles wants in. Cooper, his hands up over his head, is maxing and relaxing on the sateen sheets I bought from Filene's after watching *L.A. Confidential*. He's mysteriously without his Army of One smedium, revealing a bare chest with 7:00 a.m. shadow.

My usual early-morning MO is to throw a pillow at the door and grunt until Miles's whining gets too high-pitched to ignore. Not so today.

Dogs are either really annoying alarm clocks that you can't throw against the wall or the greatest get-out-of-bed-because-this-man-is-going-to-laze-about-your-house-all-day excuse ever invented. *Sorry, I have to take him out now.* Mood. Killed.

In truth, this was sort of the reason why I wired a woman in Arkansas a small fortune in the first place. Miles would become my furry Freud. Screw socializing: couldn't I just sit on my Ikea couch and complain my way into a relationship? Miles, unable to tell my ego from a chew toy, would never judge. *FWIW, dude, please invest in some actual therapy.* I hate Gina. She knows I don't have insurance. Also, the pound—what desperate pet adoption agencies have renamed the animal shelter—doesn't take any, which is probably a good thing. So instead of springing Spot from Alpo Alcatraz, I Googled "black pug puppy" and clicked "submit payment."

Getting a "dawg" had been a recurring dream of mine since sleeping in my first "it's just me" apartment—as in *Soooo, where are your roommates tonight? Nope, it's just me. Ma'am, if you get a second pound of tilapia, you save thirteen and a half cents. Nope, it's just me. You'll probably need two people to put this bed together, so . . . NOPE. It's. Just. Me.* Yet when I told my mother my plan to get a dog and she cooed, "Awww, are you lonely, little girl?" I was caught unawares. Lonely? I'm single, not psycho. Since loneliness is an early warning sign of schizophrenia, I decided to go for the preventive medicine. And since cats, being the harbingers of a slow friendless death, are out, my only options were dog or date.

I got Miles the next day.

After less than a month, he was already barking for his dinner. Actually it was more like a whimper, but to me it sounded just as sweet. Especially when I needed a good made-up reason to run out on the good black man chillaxing to my right. I didn't know what was wrong with me. Or maybe I just didn't care. Eight in the morning is no time for psychoanalysis. Jumping out of the wrong side of bed, I threw on my (new) dog-walking outfit—sweatpants I stole from Gina, a PHS hoodie, and fake Uggs. Cooper was muttering something about the Federal Reserve when I slipped out the door.

"She stay walking that dog," said the kid who worked on the front porch across the street. He was talking to me without talking to me. Ignoring me out loud like I usually ignore him out on the streets. His tail going off like a rudder, the dog vroomed over the asphalt. Parallel-parked his nose between the kid's boots and breathed in deep.

A BRIDGE TO NOWHERE

In the end, it was her hair that did it. Siren-songed me with its "bohemian" accent. Kind of a mix between Freddie's from *A Different World* (before the last season, when she discovers a comb) and that black girl's in *The Craft*. Brown with blond streaks that went every which-a-way. Unruly. Made my first suit—H&M with the pockets still sewn shut—look like it was trying too hard. Brown-noser. I sat with my back arched, feet crossed right over left at the ankles. She levitated for a moment above her chair, using its arms and her triceps to suspend herself in midair like a gymnast before sticking her landing on the seat Indian style. Barefoot. I could work for this woman.

Turns out, even sociopaths sometimes go shoeless.

◇◇◇◇◇◇

"Oh, my God, Helena, go get the new *Elle Décor*."

"Jeanne?"

It'd been two years, three temp jobs, and four quarters of grad school since I'd heard her voice, but I knew it right away, just like I knew exactly why she was calling. Or more specifically, whom she was calling about. We had a Super Glued bond, Jeanne and me. The stuff survivor's guilt and horror-flick romances are made of. Suffering together through something so horrendous, the two of us had nothing left to do but fall for each other and be secretly ashamed. For less than six months, we had both worked for a Manhattan interior designer with manic hair and personality to match.

"Whyyyyy . . ." I needed to hear Jeanne to bitch-slap me back to the time when we triple-fact-checked fax cover sheets and examined e-mails as if they were trace evidence against us. Back to the forty hours a week when we traded in the four elite years we'd spent being somebody for the chance to say we worked for a somebody. In some sick iteration of occupational sadomasochism, I needed her to say it . . . saaay iiit. My mouth was starting to water. Tears swarmed, and my teeth clenched. The fingernails on my free hand stabbed the lifeline there—the reading was off the charts. I was burning calories standing still.

"I've said too much already," giggled Jeanne, losing the battle to suppress more. "Just go buy it" (hee) "and turn to page 149" (hee hee).

And that was that. She hung up, and I clapped my phone closed. The nearest Borders was a three-minute power walk toward the White House. I ran like a wacko with something important to tell the president. There wasn't any time! I didn't ask about Jeanne's postapocalyptic life, and she didn't give a crap about mine.

She was the only person on the planet who knew I'd been humiliated by lack of printer ink. And I'm pretty sure I alone knew she'd spontaneously combusted over a discarded bucket of popcorn—the special holiday kind with four separate thingies for powdered cheese, red/green caramel, regular caramel, and just regular. There was a time when Jeanne knew me better than anybody. Now only her voice was familiar. Had she made it? Done what she said she would all those times we sat staring at our Mac screens, IMing each other about how much we hated one-third of our lives?

Really, this was about revenge, an emotion that most closely translates to "closure" in grown-up speak. I had a boyfriend who was so about to propose, a lead on a job with the *New York* friggin' *Times*, and in less than a month I'd have my master's degree—but Jeanne's voice took me back to the apartment in Harlem where we popped our "assistant to" cherries. When I showed up for my interview, it was Jeanne who answered the door, who said she was excited to be learning from a "successful black businesswoman," who told me this would be a great place to start. In our Ivy League remix of *Cinderella*, answering the phone by the second ring would someday transform us into CEOs. Glass ceilings were involved! She would be our fairy godmother. When the dust settled, we devolved into dum-dums every time someone forgot to turn the answering machine on. Whatever, it made sense to us then—the whole pay-your-dues thing.

And anyway, who the hell still uses answering machines? Emotionally detached (and, we guessed, sexually frustrated) interior designers who send e-mails like this:

"A properly working copier/fax/printer is essential to the basic administrative function of our office, and I expect everyone in the office to take the initiative to alert me if there is a problem or if we need to order new print cartridges. I do not expect you to wait until AFTER I've asked you to print a document for me before anything is done about it or anyone decides to mention it. Thanks."

It was the "Thanks" that got us.

She threw a temper tantrum when Jeanne and I "failed" (not forgot) to turn the machine on before escaping for lunch one day. We'd been warned. First, neither one of us had used a damned answering machine since living with our parents. Understandably, the thing was hidden away like Boo Radley. Both mesmerizing and terrifying, it was shoved way back on the bottom shelf of the one desk facing away from the front door. Nobody had to know we stocked our high-profile office with supplies from the Goodwill on 135th Street. Second, it was always so damn hard to tell whether the red light for "on" was, in fact, on. We wasted the first fifteen minutes of every lunch break quizzing each other.

"Do you think it's on?"

"I dunno. Do *you* think it's on?"

"I dunno. Do you?"

"Fucking A."

Then one of the four of us (yes, it takes four assistants to screw up an office) would martyr herself, volunteering to plant a cupped hand over the power indicator to see if it was blinking red or if the sun was trying to get us fired—again. Of course, the light wasn't on because we'd each already pushed the button two, maybe twenty, times and didn't have the superhuman powers necessary for time travel, which would've helped in figuring out whether the thing had been on in the first fucking place. After debating the issue for however long, we'd just declare the machine on and break out for lunch, gulping down spinach and avocado salads in the hopes we'd make it back before She did.

We never did.

Our final warning came one day in the "office" (the third bedroom in her rent-controlled apartment on Seventh Avenue). We'd been giddy because She was on her way to Midtown, which meant at least three hours of non-nail-biting "work" could be done. Our hopes were immediately dashed when instead of walking out the door without saying good-bye as usual, She walked into the office/bedroom with tears in her eyes. They refused to fall to her cheeks, professional that She was, but for once we weren't fooled. They were there—mucking up her huge brown eyes. The same ones that had convinced me months before that I'd be better off here. That working in a prewar building in Harlem, the same one where Spike Lee shot a few scenes of *Jungle Fever*, was the right thing to do. If the on button was that clear, we wouldn't be in this situation.

"One of you forgot to turn on the answering machine . . . again," She hissed from the doorway, not looking at anyone, so really everyone.

Blank, scared-shitless stares.

"I obviously don't know who did it," She said, still gazing up at the ceiling as if Jesus H. Christ was going to help with the interrogating, "but if it happens one more time, someone's going to have to go. I'm not sure who. I guess you guys can just decide amongst yourselves or something."

Was She just being the crazy we'd come to know and loathe, or was She actually this upset about a bootleg answering machine? Once, She brought me into her office (the second bedroom) to tell me that She dreamed about fabric samples at night and understood that the rest of us weren't as committed: after all, it was her name after the @ of our e-mail addys. I walked out thinking how lazy I was and didn't IM Jeanne for more than an hour. Then I did something wrong, and She wrote back, "I've explained several times that you have to send correspondence/ attachments to my other e-mail account. Thanks." If I couldn't make it with her, then with who?

Only once did I get something right. Looking at the Post-it

that proved it kept me sane: from going postal, if you will. It was stuck to the invoice to end all invoices. I spent all morning on it. The extra spaces between each letter of her name (added for aesthetics) were symmetrical. The design fee was hiked up to ridiculous, and the whole thing was typed in the passive voice, a tone so impersonal She could have written it herself. The invoice was placed back in my in-box with a two-by-two diploma attached—"Great Job!" Jeanne took a Polaroid as a joke. I laughed when everybody else did, then tacked it to the bulletin board above my computer. Congratulatory punctuation validated my existence. Maybe we should have checked the machine one more time.

After explaining why someone needed firing, She left us there with our empty mouths open. We didn't defend ourselves or each other. The front door slamming echoed back to us, the ending bell. Still we waited—me, Jeanne, Valentina (who actually was an idiot), and Laura (who just acted like one). Minutes passed before anyone said anything, before anyone breathed.

"Do you think she's serious?" whined Valentina, whom I mentally nominated to be thrown to the She wolf.

"Ummm, no. She's just tryna drive us insane," answered Jeanne.

"Mission a-fucking-ccomplished." This was me, obviously.

"God, I gotta get out of here," sighed Laura, who lost it one day when I left a sweaty glass on the antique desk in the living room. It left what I thought was an unnoticeable water mark. Laura hid it under a stack of papers whenever She came around.

That was our life from 9:00 a.m. to 5:00 p.m.—a constant roller coaster of wondering whether we'd do something stupid enough to get canned or so stupid we thought we deserved it. Like the day I took a retard pill and said I had nothing to do after She asked why I was so chatty with Jeanne. Backpedaling, I explained that usually my "list" was finished before the end of day, thus leaving plenty of time to giggle about bestiality Web sites with Jeanne (don't judge). I thought this explanation made me look efficient and task-oriented. It's not like I copped to the countless cups of peach tea I drank in order to have something to do in the bathroom for five minutes every hour. Despite its growing necessity, I never put peeing on my list.

The "list" arrived in our in-boxes each morning in response to a bullet-pointed e-mail we sent at the end of each day with the subject line "update." In it were punchy action verbs that justified our presence in her home:

UPDATE MAY 30, 2002

- Called Savafieh at 12:55 p.m. and the rug should arrive by 4 p.m. on July 9th

- Received Farrow & Ball samples via FedEx and placed them in your box

- Made reservations at Ouest for three at 8:30 p.m.

- Wrote responses for the Japanese article and placed them in your box for review

- Your mother called at 3:53 p.m. and she would like for you to call her back

The trick was to write things down as soon as you did them, no matter how dumb it felt. Otherwise you might forget and then end up scrounging for bullet points at around 4:58 p.m. and have only four or five on there. Ten was ideal. We saved each of our "updates" in a desktop file labeled by the month and year. After She got our update, she'd e-mail us back the "list," which laid out all our to-dos for the day and made it possible for the four of us to never have to speak to her directly. AOL was the Great Oz of our office.

Adding to the office intrigue was "the box." We each had one, and in it She placed the still-bleeding documents we'd offered up as sacrifice. This is how it went—send update, get list, write out some rando fax cover sheet from list, place in her box, e-mail her that cover sheet had been placed in her box, wait ten minutes, IM Jeanne about how stupid this is, get e-mail that revised sheet is back in your box, walk three feet to box, pick up sheet with red marker seeping through to the back, and start at go.

It's no surprise then that we became totally obsessed with her personal life. Someone that automatic couldn't just switch it off at quitting time. What were her friends like? Could we have been friends if we didn't know her secret identity? One of us heard She was dating a landscaper, and the rest immediately got busy imagining their life together. Right when I was Googling his name, She appeared at my shoulder, handing over her Palm for syncing. She never said anything about it, so obviously it was true. We figured they'd make great lawn-mowing babies. Also, She filed her family photos with the rest of the business stuff, which we thought was weird until her mom called and Jeanne picked up the phone. They chatted for a few seconds about how things were going. The old lady ended with what we thought was advice: "Remember, everything that glitters isn't gold." Now we'd found at least one piece of the puzzle, even after we each got this:

"As you know, I always call in several times a day for my phone messages, even while I'm in production. Yesterday afternoon my mother called the office to let me know that she and my father had arrived safely home from their trip. Who spoke to her and why didn't I get the message? I didn't get this message when I called in at five or five thirty p.m., and it was not included in anyone's updates."

Your mother hates you! Why do you care whether or not she made it back okay? And who even cares about stuff like that?

This isn't the 1800s. Cruise ships don't get lost at sea. Plus, it wasn't me who took the message.

The filing cabinet became our own private rabbit hole—we'd jump in whenever we got bored with the tedium of message-taking and try to make sense out of a world of hot air. Legend had it that Jeanne once found a letter in an unmarked folder from a famous black actor She dated—briefly. Simply put, according to Jeanne, it was a Dear John letter in reverse. I felt sorry for her sometimes, wondering if all She really needed was someone to love. If a strong black woman just couldn't catch a break. I was twenty-two, dating a West Point grad, and feeling authoritative in my head. She was thirty-seven, running out of time, and filing her dates. But sympathy was way too close to forgiveness. So I clung to that story like a threadbare security blanket, desperate for confirmation that the slights we felt were real.

Take the morning routine, for instance. There are some people who live and die by the chipper morning salutation. Despite being raised every morning on Frances's "You've got to ri-ise and shi-ine and give God the glory, glory," I am not one of these people. And needless to say neither was She. But damn, can a sista get a "Hi"? Sometimes we got a half-eaten "Hello," given grudgingly as She fumbled through whatever paper was in her hand at the time, and considered ourselves lucky. That's why I decided that finishing my list early and trolling the Internets for crazy animal-loving freak shows was not only totally indicative of my commitment to hard work but also remuneration for her social retardness. She didn't think so.

"Yesterday you mentioned that you often have nothing to do (other than what I have given you on your list that day). I will assume that this means that you have completed everything for my upcoming NBC segment on bedding and pillows—research in terms of identifying new resources, trends, who will loan us things for the segment, etc. Please put all of this completed information in my box for me to review at the end of the day. Thanks."

How awesome would it've been if I replied, "You're welcome," and then high-kicked my way out the front door? Too bad I opened that Platinum Student MasterCard senior year.

Funny, it was a credit card that eventually swiped Jeanne's job.

The boss lady decided that working from home wasn't working for her anymore and wasted no time renting a one-bedroom apartment on Madison Avenue near the Met. The assistants set up shop in what was formerly known as the living room, and She worked out of the bedroom. The day we moved on up, She instructed via "the list" how to orchestrate the placement of furniture, tea bags, dishes, files, Jo Malone candles, topiaries, and books. Turning on the heat somehow got left off. It was past January. We stuffed our office chairs with puffy coats and ham-handed at our keyboards with gloves on for hours before realizing how ridiculous we looked. Adrienne sent me an e-mail about unacceptable working conditions, and we decided to grab breakfast across the street at E.A.T.

E.A.T. is a fancy acronym for stupidly expensive deli. A plate of scrambled eggs and bacon was like $15. She ate there once in a while but made it a point to complain about the high price of breakfast. When we went, Whoopi Goldberg was waiting two people in front of us on line. Made me think of that line in *The Color Purple*—"This side last a lil' while, Ms. Sophia. Heaven last always." Jeanne said we should use our corporate credit cards for breakfast since (a) we were obviously suffering in unacceptable working conditions, and (b) that basically made this a business expense. Made sense to me. Pass the jelly.

She lost her shit when she got our bills. We'd been typing all morning with mittens on, which is to say really, really carefully. Wouldn't anybody with a beating heart have let it slide? It's not like we bought something that would accrue in value. It was breakfast, for grape jelly's sakes.

The next week Jeanne got called into the bedroom office via the phone intercom: "I need you back here. Thanks." We exchanged a brief glance as she got up to walk through the kitchen and into whatever shit storm She had in store. At two years, she was the veteran of the bunch. None of us were positive this was about eating at E.A.T., but we'd learned never to hope. Jeanne came back into the living room office with a smile so big I thought maybe she'd gotten promoted to like "head assistant" or something.

"She fired me."

"Whaaaa?"

"Yep."

"Are you okay?"

"Finally."

If I had been a better twenty-two-year-old, I would have left with her in some valiant display of loyalty. Instead, I watched her go and prayed I wouldn't be next. Because for all our collective bitching, I still wanted this maniac to think me worthy of another "Great Job!" Really, I just wanted her to look me in the fucking eye. So even after She made me write her a check for $15, I managed to smile through reading this:

"Received your check for your AmEx charge. Please leave $15.00 cash in my box instead (I will rip up the check). As I explained to you before, if you make any additional personal purchases on the corporate card, you will no longer be able to continue working here. If you are still unclear about this for some reason, you should read page 34 of the office policy that was given to you on Friday."

There was something missing at the bottom. I was in a no-thanks land.

Without Jeanne there to complain to, to commiserate with, it was all I could do to last through lunch. Whatever happened after was anyone's guess. I stopped trying—because despite all my fuckups, I *had* been trying. Now if my update was longer than four bullet points, I was having a good day. Messages weren't purposely forgotten, but they weren't purposefully written down either. Up until then, I'd made it one of my duties to shout "Hello" as loudly as possible when She walked through the door in order to (1) point out how crappy She was at saying it and (2) maintain my own human decency like how Tom Hanks paints a bloody face on a volleyball in *Cast Away*. Now whenever She came in, I commenced a staring match between me and my computer screen. It made my eyes hurt, and it was worth it.

In the end, in the Clue game of my life, it was the HP Inkjet, in the office, with a forgotten résumé, that did me in.

I'd been working double duty as a production assistant on her television show (I made the mistake of looking for my name in the credits once) and as her unofficial in-house scribe. Whenever someone e-mailed her, asking her expert advice, I was the one who wrote back. It was the only worthy experience of my day, and I stretched a hundred-word reply on the correct pronunciation of "chaise" to take at least two hours. That's around the time I realized what I wanted to do and started trolling Monster.com for gigs that had "write" in the title. What got me wasn't the faxing out of my résumé during work hours. Who doesn't do that? What got me was the copy of my résumé left in the machine overnight.

Again with the phone intercom. "Helena, can you come back here?" Maybe she wanted to congratulate me for looking for another job. I'd made it perfectly clear that I had an English degree that I planned on using. She even said that this would be a great opportunity for that, since, you know, She was so "well-connected."

In fact, her best friend was the editor of a magazine. I overheard them once talking on the phone, talking about doing their own laundry at a coin-operated 'mat, and figured I was golden. Until I wasn't. I guess She didn't think I would ever actually try to make it. That filling my heart with hate every day would be fulfilling.

She was barefoot once again. I took a seat on the chair facing her without being offered and crossed my legs dramatically, all Sharon Stone in *Basic Instinct*, trying my hardest to act like I was interrogating her (it works for interviews).

"I was looking in the fax machine last night and found this," She said with such dinner-theater emphasis on the word *this* that I almost let out a gasp when she flipped over the wayward copy of my résumé lying facedown on the coffee table. Is She for real? My résumé? I thought She'd printed out all the orange-alert e-mails I'd sent to Adrienne and Gina about how "fucking psycho" She was.

"Okaaaaay." To keep my face looking serious, I stared at the space between her eyebrows. "You *do* know that I want to write, right?" Ending a declarative sentence with the mocking inflection of a question. Perfect. I was handling this like a *Law and Order* extra.

"This is unacceptable, Helena. You won't be able to continue working for us. We're going to have to ask you to leave." It was the first time She acknowledged her many personalities. And for the first time in six months, I felt like she might have actually gotten a glimpse of me.

"That's fine," I replied, faster than I thought professional, but I couldn't help it. I'se free nah! "Do I have to stay all day, or can I leave now?" She looked away. Her wild curls wilted.

Still pinching my deserted résumé, She mumbled something about finishing up anything outstanding on my list. My eyes were still rolling when I sat back down at my desk, ready to write my final update. It only took ten minutes and two spell checks to come up with this:

Dear She,

I believe that all working relationships should end with an evaluation. I would like to say that I enjoyed my experience here, but sadly I cannot. Your complete lack of managerial skills and overall menacing demeanor are key factors in my displeasure here at your company.

To send blatantly rude e-mails and end them with a mocking "thanks" is not only rather childish, but totally unbefitting of a senior manager. On a personal note, to enter a room and offer a rather weak and mumbled "hello" and to communicate entirely by e-mail in a rather small office are behaviors indicative of one who does not value sociable relationships with his/ her employees, which is clearly distinctive of this office and totally antithetical to a congenial work environment.

Lastly, to treat your employees with not only a nonchalant manner, but actual disdain, is offensive and the foremost reason this office has an alarmingly high employee turnover rate. I say these things because I believe you should cultivate the qualities that are befitting of a true leader in order to have a successful business and life.

I am pleased to be moving forward to a position where my talents are not only properly utilized but appreciated. I sincerely hope that you find the necessary characteristics to enjoy normal business relations with your employees and colleagues, who for the most part are severely dissatisfied with your simply mean behavior.

I hope this helps,
Helena Andrews

Bad. Ass. The guts to read it aloud to her face would have been nice, but I settled for the grammar skills. In reality I didn't have another job lined up, but there was no reason for her to know that. The letter was my first grown-up resignation. Once the send button was fired, including a few names in the BCC field, I made a beeline for the front door and never looked back— that is, until Jeanne decided to call me two years later with news.

The trip down trauma lane didn't take long at all. I'd snapped out of it by the time I got to the magazine section, scanning the titles for *Elle Décor*. I could've just skipped through the pages right then and there and gotten it over with, all dirty like. But I didn't want randos around when I saw whatever it was Jeanne wanted me to see. This was a private moment. I bought my copy and ran to a storefront across the street.

Page 149, please tell me something good, or at the very least something so depraved it makes me smile. And there She was. Her hand was on her hip, and the other was resting "naturally" against the fireplace in her living room. Gone was the desk with my water-glass stain. She had on a heavily bejeweled tank dress, probably from Bendel's. Her biceps were as muscular as I remembered. I could even tell without my glasses that her fingernails had been manicured—French—and She was wearing that nude lip gloss. She looked like your mom's cool younger sister visiting from the big city for the weekend. Why couldn't things have worked out between us? I like the big city. I like weekends.

But one of these things was not like the other. Something was . . . missing. Oh, fuck! Where her hair should've been, there was . . . nothing. Not a hat or hijab. She was bald as the day she was born, if, in fact, she had been.

I stared at that image for the devil knows how long, wishing it wasn't true and glad that it was. I closed the magazine and carefully slipped it back into my purse. There was a brief moment of silence before I called everyone who knew what She'd put me through, feeling a twinge of shame each time I phoned another friend but forcing it down. "One word. Four syllables. Alopecia." The more times I said it, the more sadistic I started to sound, sort of like She did when the couch pillows weren't karate-chopped just so. Her hair was gone, sure, but maybe it was my moral fiber that was receding. Maybe that's what Jeanne wanted me to see.

So in the end end, the for-real end, the no-more-sequels end— it was the hair that got me.

CHASING MICHELLE

There's something terribly frightening about being the only black person at a political newspaper when there's a black guy running for president. Or should I say freeing? Whatever F word you choose, I was most likely fucked.

It was like the Christmas story on steroids: a random act of birth had suddenly bestowed upon me a type of divine wisdom. Running low on Frankincense and myrrh, melanin would have to do. "You should totally be out on the trail right now," a colleague would say.

"Why, because I'm black?"

"Well, yeah."

"I'll take it."

I finally felt special—or maybe I didn't, finally. Either way, I knew covering Hillary's pantsuits wouldn't get me on someone's masthead. So when my bosses at *Politico* needed someone to go down south to get the "black perspective" on then-Sen. Barack

Obama's possible primary win, I ditched the "who gives a fuck" act and started packing.

This was big shit. At last I'd see some return on my grad-school investment. Once I got to the *Times*, the previous year I'd spent mastering journalism at Northwestern felt like a setup to this highly sophisticated field study of the overeducated black female in the bull pen. I lived and died by the phone. Some days I got over myself by timing how fast I could pass out newspapers, shuffle through faxes, and sort bins of mail. The scene that follows is real. The characters therein are not actors, but actual people:

The main phone line at the news desk rings. The caller ID shows a three-digit number. The assistant knows it's in-house but answers the phone with the standard company greeting, anyway. She's a consummate professional. Whatever that means.

NEWS ASSISTANT: Times?! [*it's both invitation and edict*]

A1 REPORTER: HelenaBritanyaPolly?

ASSISTANT [*all too used to the tripled moniker*]: Helena. What can I do you for?

REPORTER [*serious tone*]: I seem to have found myself in italics.

ASSISTANT [*bemused*]: Whaaaaa?

REPORTER: Suddenly everything I type is in italics, and I can't get out.

ASSISTANT [*still trying to maintain professional decorum*]: Well, how did you get in?

REPORTER: No idea.

ASSISTANT [*sighs, thinking about the amount she owes in loans*]: Control. I.

What I needed to control was my work rage—a swirling typhoon that sucked whatever front-page hopes I had down to my gut, threatening to explode out the business end. The "in case of idiocy" affirmation went like this: (deep inhale) (slow exhale) ramen noodles, plastic forks, Ivy League, master's degree, NYT, ramen noodles, plastic forks . . . Mentally fast-forwarding through all the boring stuff in order to one day get to the good parts helped some. The speech I'd give at a prestigious podium would undoubtedly mention Frances. Once that got old, I'd already gotten a few stories in the paper—even wrote five hundred words on Muslim women being cool with the whole hijab thing for the A section. Eventually, five stories in fourteen months would forever spoil me for the title of assistant and earn me a job at the *Politico* covering political news (yuck) in Virginia (yuck yuck).

Fine, the joke was on me—"Wait, I thought you wanted to do arts and culture stuff? Do you even know where the Capitol is, dude?"—but I planned to make the most of it. During one of his cigarette breaks, Mr. Leary, a reporter from the *Times* who actually knew my name, gave me some advice: "Kid, you always gotta look two jobs ahead." I loved it when he called me kid. It was so . . . authentic. He'd given me a pocket-sized can of pepper spray after I'd been mugged for the second time walking home from the bureau late at night. He made me promise only to whip it out if I seriously planned on using it; otherwise the suspect in question could always use it against me. He also said it didn't work on "Latinos," but I forgave him that. Two jobs from now, I'd parlay covering history into covering Hollywood, where I wouldn't need no stinking pepper spray.

In short, screwing this Barack thing up would mean a lifetime (e.g., another year) of watching grainy reruns of the unfunny version of *Saved by the Bell* that is the legislative branch of the U.S. government, with Harry Reid as the cantankerous but lovable Mr. Belding. If you can picture Mr. Belding better than you can majority leader Sen. Harry Reid (D-Nev.), then like me, you should never be in possession of a congressional press pass.

But there was one snag on my red carpet to the Pulitzers. It was becoming increasingly impossible to disguise my violent allergic reaction to the phrases "on the Hill," "in session," "staffer profile," "pushing the envelope," and "pulling back the curtain." "I hate everyone" became my new "Good morning." How could I convince the bosses I avoided at Chipotle that I could be a chip off the old block?

There was a new features editor. Over coffee, I convinced him that someone needed to go to South Carolina, and that that someone could only be me. I never actually pulled the race card per se, but I'd never cut it in two with a pair of scissors in front of unsuspecting diners either. We got into logistics after I got the official go-ahead—like where I was going to stay, how I was going to get around Columbia, and who the hell I was going to talk to. They wanted "reax" from regular folks, who couldn't be hard to find.

During the Friday plane ride, my idle thoughts got some exercise jumping ahead to Monday morning in the office, when the story would be front page, be on Drudge, and then get bandied between boxes of blowhard foursquare on cable. I do this a lot— sneak into advanced screenings of my life. But the trailers for *Helena Does South Carolina* were totally misleading. Instead of an intellectual thriller, this thing would turn out to be a romantic tragedy.

It started with an old man loitering in a "garage."

The plan was simple—grab a handful of the pulsating masses of black people brimming on southern streets and get them to say something profound. Also, I can't drive—as in don't know how. Frommer's was moderately helpful in finding me a "car service" to get me to my hotel. At the airport, a balding white guy in a leather bomber jacket was flashing a sign that read "Andrews." We were surprised to see each other. He sounded black on the phone, and I could tell he assumed I wasn't.

"Whatchu heah foh," he asked, lifting my carry-on into the back of his "cab"—a black Lincoln-like town car with a laptop where the meter should have been. Littered with yellowing newspapers and what I assumed were conspiracy theorist manifestos, the entire front seat looked as if it belonged to either someone just too busy to make it to the recycling center or a deranged psycho killer.

I got in anyway.

"I'm a journalist, and I'm doing a story on Senator Barack Obama."

"Uh-huh."

"Actually, you might be able to help me. Is there a particular neighborhood or any place down here where African Americans hang out?"

"Oh. Well, you don't wanna be going to any of those places. It ain't rally safe—drugs and . . ." The rest of that sentence would only be important to know at my murder trial. I'm not going to say "Mr. Cabdriver, sir" was a racist, but he was racist-ish. After a mind-boggling minutes-long tirade about all the places I shouldn't go because "the blacks"—who he personally had nothing against— in Columbia were not only dangerous but also totally in the dark about politics, he dropped me off at the one place he knew there'd be "someone smert enough tuh talk tuh ya," Dr. Ray's Used Cars and Ground Transportation. He promised I'd be safe.

"They'll take care of you," he said, now unloading the trunk, perhaps unaware of the alarming similarity his guarantee had to a gangster's. Perhaps. "It's back in there." He pointed to a darkened wormhole–slash–front door near where his "Lincoln" was parked. You've got to be shitting me.

But before I had the chance to plead, "Wait, what? In there?!" the handle to my suitcase was in my hand, and I was left alone, listening to the popping sounds tires make when they run over busted-up gravel mixed with dirt. Across the driveway, overalled men worked under the huge shadows of beached Beemers. It started to rain, and I walked inside.

See, this is what Gina calls "some ole white people stuff." The type of commonsense-defying idiocy—sticking your head in a "trained" lion's mouth, walking alone from the train at 2:00 a.m.—that we of the overcritical-black-female variety routinely categorize as "white girl shit." Which is to say any action that is in no way demonstrative of how we ourselves personally would behave in a situation of similar life-threatening level. Much is made of the high mortality rate of horror-movie black people. But think of it as a question of plot, not prejudice. Boomsheekah gets the ax in the first five minutes of *Slasher Movie Magic IV*, not because she lacks the mental acumen to stay alive, but because the whole thing would have been over in the five minutes it takes to run out the front door (not up the damn stairs) and call the police (not your idiot friend who lives twenty minutes away).

Back at the garage, nobody came out to offer me a mint julep, so after standing perfectly still with my eyeballs looping roller-coaster-like in their sockets, I decided to stop looking like an asshole and go inside. The solid smell of boiling meat greeted me at the door like a gruff old man. *Whuddayawan, I don't have all fucking day.*

"Heeehhh-looowww," I yodeled, one hand gripping the door-frame.

"Yeahp," came the answer from the next room.

I approached the main office the way a Discovery Channel intern approaches a den of wild hyenas in the bush—very care-fully and with low-pay-grade precautions. Sticking my head into the room before the rest of me followed, I wouldn't take my note-pad out just yet—don't want to frighten them into a stampede. *Them* was a seventy-one-year-old black man, J. C. Martin, and the boss of the place, "Dr. Ray" Charles Jones, who, judging from the juice of his Jheri curl, looked to be in his early fifties and definitely not a doctor.

Steak and onions. That, plus motor oil. Perfect. I was inter-rupting lunch. Everybody knows wild things act more so when they're hungry. Dr. Ray walked over to a Crock-Pot on a desk littered with garage tools, stirring what was inside before intro-ducing himself and his friend. "He'll answer all your questions," he said, nodding to where J.C. was sitting without taking his eyes off what was in the pot. I took out my reporter's notebook.

"I know more about Jesse Jackson than Obama. He just popped up. I never heard anybody say anything about no Obama," answered J.C. when I asked him the most profound question I could muster: Did you ever think you'd live to see this day? We went on like that for a while—me asking stupid ques-tions and him trying his best to answer them without making me feel stupid. He sat with his legs so far apart I was in constant uncomfortable eye contact with his old-man junk. I played it off by pretending to be blind. He wouldn't tell me what J.C. stood for, aside from "the closest you'll ever get to Jesus Christ." When it was finally over, he decided to do some interviewing of his own. Probably trying to show off.

J.C. and his wife had been married for fifty years before she died. Dr. Ray, who finally started acknowledging my presence, said he "got started early" and had eleven children before he was middle-aged. I scanned a shelf crowded with frames of cap-and-gowned girls and tuxedoed boys, while Ray checked on his steaks and onions for the third time. He mentioned his wife in the past tense, and I nodded, not sure how we got so off topic. But there does come a point after one has reached the socially preferred age of procreation when talking about one's reproductive prospects with total strangers is not only common practice, but anticipated.

"Are *you* married?" asked J.C. as I was furiously scribbling down details. Something like—"Ray Charles Jones, who runs a ground transportation business in Columbia . . ."

"Ahhhh? No," I answered hastily, looking up with a cocked eyebrow. I knew this would be coming, but not so soon. My coat was still on.

"But you're looking for a husband? Right?" This was more of a biblical command than anything else. Make babies, not bachelor's degrees.

Had I been looking? Had any of us? I wasn't so sure. At that point, Dex and I were still in the "this could so work" phase. Everything he did was magic—making inedible eggs, writing impossible poetry. Imagining the look he'd give me just as the doors were opening for my big reveal on the day of our wedding was a treasured pastime. As was examining every inch of his Facebook wall. Happy to claim somebody, I was hardly concerned if he was *that* somebody, and ignored the faraway looks he sometimes got. Besides, a stared-at BlackBerry never vibrates or whatever. If I was out there looking all the damn time, I'd probably never stop long enough to find someone. In my head that sounded all feministy and liberated and logical.

Hiding behind a brief smile, I considered what to say to the little old man sitting in front me with the potbelly and splayed knees. He was waiting patiently for whatever answer I was searching for. How exactly does one look for a husband? Is there an educational game I should've gotten for Christmas instead of Where in the World Is Carmen Sandiego? Who's got time to find Machu Picchu when there's a man on the loose?

If I had screamed, "YES, yes. A thousand times yes!" would I be better for it or worse? Of course I wanted someone of the male variety, a husband even, to help get rid of the lonelies, but hadn't I just gotten to the looking point? Or was it the tipping point? Even after reading Dex's copy of Malcolm Gladwell in four metro rides, I still didn't know the answer to that. So J.C. got the response I usually saved for family things. "I'm just way too busy. I'm trying to be a super star right now. Career stuff, you know?" It's hard to imagine three more ridiculous sentences in the history of speech. I'd either just sledgehammered more nails in the coffin of educated-while-black relationships or slugged a grand slam for the home team.

"Uh-huh," J.C. grunted, sliding down a few more inches in his chair, junk in full view. We were done here.

But there was still the question of my ride.

Ray said he knew the best young person to take me around and introduce me to black people—his oldest daughter, Rayetta. Suspicion and superiority immediately took hold of my soul.

When she arrived, she told me she was twenty-six, only a year younger than me. Her nails were long and red, and her hair was hard and crimped. She had never been on a plane before and asked me twice if police cars in Washington looked the same as the ones in Columbia. Not sure of what she meant, I answered yes.

"Can we see the stuff you write online?"

"Umm-hmm, just go to—"

"But we can get that here? On our computers in Columbia?"

Loose lawns ran into one another and past the windows of her cab (she worked for Ray during the day). She could have been one of my cousins, the ones who made me drink Listerine and still thought I lived in New York. I kept still in the backseat, silently scrolling through already-read e-mails. For whatever reason, chitchatting with her felt like a chore. Actually, I knew the reason. I didn't ask, but I guessed that she had kids. That she went to the karaoke every Friday night if there weren't any lanes left to bowl on. And that she was married, engaged, or in some other way involved with a man. Just like all the Korean girls from high school with new Facebook albums—"Jackie Kim's Wedding!" According to Gina, our best bet was to be an Asian psychology major from Biloxi. Too late. Even Gary—the slutbag I lost my virginity to in college and then was bored into dating after graduation—was getting married to a girl whose profile pic read "Cambodian."

"Her name is fucking Sue Meh," I groaned.

"Ohmigod, dude, her name is litigious."

"The Asians, that's what it's about. It's like 1989 all over again," I said, having absolutely no idea whether or not there was a violent uptick in Asian/black unions in 1989. But for some reason, it sounded about right.

"It's time, man—the marrying time. Just not for us. Not black women. We don't ever get a time. Not never." A *Waiting to Exhale* moment followed, and afterward the two of us got back to the business of living our lives.

Rayetta had probably never even seen *Waiting to Exhale*. And if she had, I'm sure she didn't know any of the lines by heart like we did. For example: "Well, guess what, John, YOU'RE the motherfuckin' improper influence!" Sitting up there in the front seat with her red-ass nails on the steering wheel, Rayetta didn't have a care in the world, because her world was about as big as a tank of gas. I should've asked her some questions while we were on our way to the hotel—it would save me some time—but I didn't want her voice in *my* piece.

Instead I made appointments with graduate students and young professionals, wrote my story, and flew home. It made the front page without Rayetta in it.

But she wasn't all gone. I finally got the courage to interview her on our way to the airport—we were running ridiculously late because she didn't realize I needed to be there more than ten minutes before my flight. For the last few days, whenever I climbed into the backseat—after she'd been waiting for me to finish asking someone more worthy what *real* regular folk felt about Obama—Rayetta would always ask how it went. I'd grumble meaningless stock sentences, and we'd take off. Once I got as far as "so . . ." but stopped myself before adding "what do you think?" Deciding I already knew her life, I felt stupid asking about it. On my way out of the South, I figured what the hell, it's not like I'll ever see her again. I acted like we were having an actual conversation while I tapped her answers into my Berry. She didn't think I was paying attention. She said her mother hosted a party for Mrs. Obama a few months back. "Michelle came to the house and served hors d'oeuvres," said Rayetta with something more than pride—familiarity maybe. "She was real nice. She sure got our vote."

This was the first time I'd felt stingy since second grade. Michelle was ours, damn it!

A black president—shrug. For those of us who didn't watch *Roots* on the first color TV ever, that always seemed possible. But a black first lady—with diplomas in plural, a career in progress, a presidential husband, and perfect babies—now that was "historical quantity." Michelle was our anchor in outer space.

Rayetta knew this, and I'd tried to ignore her. After spending years claiming to be the best black woman possible, I wasted two silent days in a backseat, afraid to talk to a real one. I left Rayetta out of my story, but kept our interview on my Berry for months.

◇◇◇◇◇◇

"I have never been more hyped to not have nobody," said Gina as we were making plans for the inauguration. She'd be in Washington for the whole week. Triple negatives aside, I was confused.

"Are you serious, dude?" Since when did single and loving it become acceptable for our "about me" sections?

"Dude, Michelle is making it super famous to be a black woman right now. I'm ready."

I guess she was right. Maybe Mrs. Obama would be our sixth man, invisibly racking up assist after assist. Maybe we'd even get laid. But Gina was the basketball star in high school. It took a year of scoring a grand total of ten points in JV until I ditched the Alonzo Mournings for a pair of pom-poms—making noise on the sidelines seemed more productive. Anyway, I was beginning to think I was unMichelle-able—at least when it came to the man I wanted most to see me as first-lady material.

During the final four of our breakup championship, Dexter called me an elitist. We argued about picket fences and my hatred for the mediocre lives they were built to prettify. That type of life disgusts me, I told him after it'd been made totally clear that he didn't want that type of life with me. We're so different, he said. You're right; I was just horny when we met. We both know this is pointless, I mean, it's not like you were ever in my league or anything. *Sweet Jesus, somebody stop me.* I want someone who'll take me to live in Malaysia or something, I said, like a Peace Corps volunteer with an endless trust fund. Because Dex didn't want to run the country with me, I decided to run him down with all the expectations I never had.

Like I say, it was frightening to be a black woman when a black woman like Michelle was around, was everywhere. And when her husband won the White House, everybody kept talking about how little black boys would have no more excuses. No father, no money, a name blacker than dirt—you too can rule the world. But no one talked (cared) about how Michelle changed us. We'd lain awake nights wondering if our Wonder Woman acts would ever get found out. Then suddenly there was proof we could be everyday and superhuman. But where were the instructions?

Still, Gina was weirdly positive that all this would work in our favor, and I was still scared shitless—this could be a train wreck waiting to happen. But like a rubbernecking driver on the freeway, I couldn't take my eyes off her.

Michelle does weird things with her lips sometimes. When she's waiting for someone to finish asking her a question or just waiting for someone to shut up, she folds her mouth in on itself just briefly, like she's warming it up or something. What comes out next—you know it's going to be good.

She was on *The View* once, televising the revolution. While Barbara Walters stuttered on about something or other, there it was again. Michelle's lips pressing against each other as if getting ready for a smack or a smack-down.

"People aren't used to strong women." She was talking about her husband's opponent, Sen. Hillary Clinton, but this was all about me. Usually the people who think the people on TV are talking to them are straitjacketed. I, on the other hand, couldn't be saner. "We don't even know how to talk about 'em," she continued, wearing a $148 dress from White House/Black Market. Rayetta could get that dress.

I bought a J. Crew dress that looked like something she'd wear—sheath, cobalt blue, understated. Once, I was in a car packed mostly with women when the one guy, a friend of mine, almost got killed. "Michelle isn't even all that cute," he said. "She got a really high booty." By some miracle he made it out in one piece. But the truth is, she isn't the most beautiful woman in the world. Her butt does sit up kind of high. She's a "dark, black, woman," as Whoopi put it that day on *The View*, slapping the back of her hands together to slam home the meaning of each of those adjectives.

I don't think Michelle minds being our new muse. I think she gets it. We little brown girls—drunk off *The Cosby Show*, sobered up by life, and a little suicidal—we need her.

These days the word *hope* is unsuitable for civilized conversation, having been ridden hard and put away so wet on the campaign trail. But despite being the vocabulary equivalent of a slutbag, there's no better word to describe Michelle's spot in our run-down hearts.

Gina's even got a new pickup line to be used during our inauguration-weekend festivities: "I have a master's degree. Fuck me."

"PERFECT GIRL"

AND OTHER CURSE WORDS

He meant it as an insult.

Maybe if he called me a "stuck-up bitch whose sadistic obsession with a mythological black male would inevitably leave her childless," maybe then I could've slapped him like a monochromatic movie star before slinking off to the boudoir to be "ahvown."

Instead he called me "perfect girl," and I was forced to snuggle up to the rented space between his bicep and his pits, breathing in the stink of another relationship gone bad. Perfect girl? I gave us another month. Two, tops.

First you have to know that Dex already had a growing urban harem of "girls." There was "hotel girl," "club girl," "seven-month school girl," "London girl," "law school girl," and a girl whose secret identity I knew but whom I refused to refer to as anything other than "Prom Shoes." Actually, I knew the etymology of each one, because so far, I'd been losing at a little game I play called

"Super Cool," in which I pretend to be the super coolest girl in the history of the universe, so cool, in fact, that it's totally cool for us to chat about all your other so-called relationships because "it's cool, my baby," and we both know that in the end you'll choose me, the coolest. Despite sucking at sports, I keep at it.

The toughest part of my favorite pastime is making sure the other player never catches on to how I really feel. Keeping secret that one more word about Prom Shoes' (the only one of Dex's girls who I'd seen in real life, in silvery rhinestoned peep toes) complete lack of moral authority as evidenced in her choice of footwear might send me to the other team, Red Rover style—sweaty, pissed, and eventually submissive.

Even with all that pent-up obsession, when the time came for my comic book christening I used my amazing super powers to keep my mouth shut. It happened like the Fortune Cookie game where the future always tastes better "in bed." We were lying on one, stretching out my Jersey sheets with 3:00 a.m. predictions of what might come next for us. For me, it was a life made painless by the proximity of another human being. For Dex, it was probably another blow job, the possibility of which brought him to his next point.

"Wanna know what our code word for you is?" he whispered to the ceiling that night as I lay naked by his side, trying to make a permanent impression of my 34Bs on his chest—a physiological proof of purchase. Staring down at his other head, I was immediately grateful he couldn't see me smiling like a dismembering serial killer. *Our?* He talked about me with his friends? *Code word?* I was worthy of synecdoche?! Some lucky part of me (bitchy, baby-hungry, black?) was going to be the immortal epithet to my issues with men. If I'd paid more attention to Mrs. Paul's sixth-grade lecture on word choice, I'd know whether to be anxious or eager.

"Whaaaaaaaat?" I sighed, hoping to sound appropriately apathetic and not like the possessed Dex fiend that I'd become. *Umm, he already knows, dude.* By then it'd been about a month, and already everything about him gave me uncontrollable ghost itch—his love of the History Channel and skinny neckties. I would call it something paranormal if this hadn't been the natural flow of things: girl meets boy, boy says something awkwardly amusing to girl, girl decides boy must be *him*, and then Facebook turns him into a hobby—or a habit. I was addicted, and *our* code word would be my next fix.

"Perfect girl," he said in the dark.

Fuck. I stretched the ashen webbing between my toes to their limit, arched my back to the point of breaking, and dug my nails a few centimeters deeper into his man boobage. But this wasn't ecstasy, it was exhaustion.

I'd spent the last thirty days doing everything to prove myself worthy of calling this jackass my boyfriend. When Dex called me at 3:00 a.m. wanting to talk about nothing in particular (but really everything indefinable), I answered the phone (which had been waiting impatiently beneath my pillow). When Dex wanted dinner, I cooked as if I hadn't ordered the No. 17 from Sala Thai for the last six nights in a row. When his number showed up on my BlackBerry in the middle of a Tuesday (ice cream at the Lincoln Memorial!), I slapped an end quote on the ass of another boring story and ran outside to meet him. I even had an "in case of Dex" bag under my desk at work (mascara, thongs, Burt's Bees, invisible solid). I washed his dishes while mine nurtured micro universes at home. I did his laundry while going pantyless by necessity. I gently lectured him on fiscal responsibility while waiting in line at ACE Check Cashing and Pay Day Loans.

In short it was no surprise, then, that when given the Rorschach test of premeditated shit I never do, the suicidal adjective that leaped from Dex's lips was "perfect." This was an involuntary response based on shoddy research, like having a panic attack after a missed period. Just wait a couple more days. What shocked me was that he'd actually bought it. He seriously believed that he'd found the Ivy League Barbie Doll, the fully posable collector's edition complete with removable panties. No wonder Frances refused to buy me those monsters as a kid. It wasn't about the impossible complex I'd develop—to be young, gaunt, and blond—but the all-too-possible fulfillment of that fantasy. I could and would be perfect for this perfect man, my Ken without the plastic hair. The thing is, I was, and he wasn't. So I resented, and he retreated. That night, he thought explaining himself would break the awkward silence he didn't expect. (I mean, who doesn't want to be "perfect girl"?)

"You are actually better than me as a person," he confessed, unnecessarily. "If we had a person contest, you would defeat me—handily."

"Are you serious?" I answered back, trying to sound both flattered and surprised, but definitely not scared shitless.

"Yeah, I mean, you're awesome."

Like I said, Dexter didn't know it yet, but with one word he'd begun to seal our fate, activating the ticking time bomb on the dating doomsday device. Perfect girl? Depending on which side of the law you were on, she was either superhero or villain. By now it should be apparent to most that I am neither perfect nor any synonym thereof. Moreover, at this exact moment in time I've realized that playing Super Cool is not a good look, because despite my very best efforts, I'd become a girl, not *the* girl. Really, I was one of *those* women—the ones who are so strong and black that the jumbo-size *S* on their chests is assumed. I for one don't remember the trip to the phone booth.

Actually, that's a lie.

It's like how I figured out how to cheat at FreeCell.

I discovered the game one virgin night in my freshman dorm room, JJ 602. Mousing through My Computer seemed more gratifying than reading more Virgil. Minesweeper, being the most asinine guessing game ever invented, was out of the question. Hearts is for a demographic who don't know nothing 'bout no computers. And Solitaire? Too obvious.

FreeCell I'd never tried. The mug shot of the bearded blond king guarding the game had misled me all these PC years. He was staring offscreen somewhere, perhaps into the blank page that was my social life. I read it as a warning sign but double-clicked anyway, spending the next four hours pairing black queens with red kings and forgetting about the fact that some jackass hadn't called. Highlighting the arrow of All Programs to Accessories, which led to Games, which then pointed to FreeCell, made me feel like I was going somewhere. Having unblemished stats made me feel like it didn't matter that I wasn't. If a single round seemed lost, before giving up I'd walk away from the computer, take a lap around the sixth floor, maybe even have a conversation with a human being, and then come back—mind cleared and ready to rock. At the height of my lameness, I had a streak of like 27 wins and 0 losses, which is not to say that I only played 27 games of FreeCell. If I ever lost—no matter how geekily high my win column—I'd take a final glance at the awesomeness of my achievement and start over. "Are you sure you want to clear all statistics?" Yes. Eventually, I got sloppy, got my cherry popped, and left FreeCell behind with all my other freshman things.

When real life happened, the idea of stealing a few minutes from work doing something mindless became as compulsory as a cigarette break. This time around, however, losing was not an option. Half-finished games would stay minimized at the bottom of my screen for days, the bearded king looking militaristic. Stumbling into a statistical loophole that ensured I'd never "lose" made me feel more genius than cheat.

Say all the free cells are loaded. A Queen of Spades is propped up against a King of Diamonds. Just one column over is a lonely King of Hearts. She's sort of got options—one egomaniac for another—but then again, not really. So the game's over, technically— but, since there are pointless moves left, not really. At this point, there's nothing else to do but stare at the screen and wish you had made better choices in the beginning, right? Not quite. If you ever find yourself stuck between that Queen of Spades and no place (that is to say, in royal trouble), relax. Just make sure you save all the really important crap you have up—Excel spreadsheets entitled "HDA Expenses: The Musical Comedy," and PDFs of party invites you'll never rsvp to—and then go to your start menu and end it all. I mean shut the shit down. For some holy reason, the "Are you sure you want to resign this game?" box doesn't pop up. And best of all, when you log back in to Windows, FreeCell won't count your cowardice as a loss—just a temporary breakdown.

That's what Dex was. Or, better yet, that's who perfect girl was. Just a momentary lapse in perception. The game, not being lost or over, just needed a reboot. Pretending perfect works just as good as being. If I showed him the Michelle in me, then eventually he'd have to see the Helena in me too. She's creeping around here somewhere—crouched down behind the trash cans blocking my basement apartment's window, sneaking peeks at the two happy people clicking between History Channel and HGTV. One is dreaming of a "three, two" somewhere in Silver Lake, and he's boning up on the big bang theory. One time, they both got really crazy and started Googling Chicago real estate. The perfect girl almost had a seizure. He was just having a spousal moment. It would eventually pass, though, and the window to the basement apartment would get blocked by too many recycling bins.

The same conversation got rinsed, reprocessed, and repurposed every few weeks:

"I'm just scared I can't live up to even your lowest expectations of me," Dex announced to the back of my head on another night for insomniacs.

"I'm sorry . . . what?" Remember, alls I had to do was reboot without regret, and none of this would count in the morning. I was only half listening.

"I don't know." He sighed, using one hand to wipe down his face like a clean slate. "It's like you're perfect, you put everything like out there and do everything right. What do I do besides screw everything up?"

"I have no clue how to respond to that without violence."

"You're like my favorite verse. I've got you on repeat and I never get tired of you, but . . ."

"So just to review—" I had to stop the hip-hop similes before Jeeps got involved. "You're saying that I'm too good for you."

"I don't know. Something like that. I'm just bad with women."

I exhaled resignation, flipped over so my back faced his front, and scooted my ass deeper into the crook of his crotch. "Go to sleep," I said, shutting him down. Tomorrow we'd start up again, and maybe then I'd figure out a way to win. And if this was a blinking warning signal, then Gina was the pop-up message that spelled everything out, "Sorry, you lose. There are no more legal moves."

"If dude is telling you fifty thousand ways that he ain't ready, listen to him," she concluded at the end of a marathon my-life-sucks-and-every-dude-I-date-turns-out-to-be-a-raging-asshole phone call. She was probably right, but 'member before what *he* said? He *said* I was perfect. Remember that? Can't we just focus on that for a minute, please?

Gina had memories of my own to share. Like when West Point Willy told me he wanted to "take a step back," and I let him date other women, knowing he'd come back to me one day because, *hellooo*, I was the best thing that'd ever happened to him since not dying in Iraq. I wasn't, and he didn't. And when Abdul said he wasn't over his ex-fiancée and I gave him time, because seriously, that chick was hideous, and he, despite being Muslim, bought me a DVD player for Christmas. Like if he could barrel through religious roadblocks as hard-core as Islam versus whatever I was, then forgetting some hideola girl who wore jean skirts should not be that hard. They got back together in three months, and I got Netflix. And when James said he thought he would lose his job shuffling legal briefs because I worked in the newsroom twenty-one floors down, I thought he was totally justified. The plan was to just wait until he went back to school in the fall. September came and went. He started dating some midget who ran marathons and, according to Facebook, liked cooking "big ole meals."

Gina had points.

"We broke up last night," was how I said hello the next morning. I gave up on being perfect and decided to be a soldier instead. I blocked Dex on IM. I threw the toothbrush I kept at his apartment in *his* trash can, hoping the pathetic image would drive him insane, or at least to my basement apartment on Ninth Street.

"Whaaaaa?" Gina said, feigning an appropriate modicum of surprise. Best friend indeed.

"Yeah, dude. He said he wasn't ready for a relationship and bla bla bla. We're done this time. I can't do this back-and-forth shit anymore. It's for the birds."

"Right, dude, you gotta keep that shit moving." She was on auto-pilot now. "K.I.M."

We both knew this was all bullshit—a rehearsed spontaneous dance number that was getting harder to perform night after night. I was the jerk in the Magical Mister Mistoffelees costume wondering how my master's in fine arts came to this. Dex was the master of backtracking. My phone rang by evening. Maybe he'd come around—the white-capped mountains of my gleaming perfection. Maybe it was snow blindness he was scared of, not a healthy, loving, and monogamous relationship with one Helena "You're Awesome, You're Perfect, Now Change" Andrews. How would I ever know if I didn't pick up the phone? "Hello?" We're back "together" in the time it takes to spell-check *abracadabra*.

I was an annoying narrative arc on a teen soap opera. Okay, we get it. These two crazy kids will never get together! It's impossible. Too much has happened! Dan and Serena, I'm bored of you now. The best way to flip the script would be to get the upper hand this time. I never IM'd Dex first. Let the phone ring at least three times before answering. And I refused to play Scrabulous with him for weeks, ignoring every new game he started and then pretending like I hadn't. I was through with games, see.

"Stop ignoring my Scrabulous requests!"

"What are you talking about, crazy pants?"

"My pants aren't crazy. Get on Scrabulous."

Obviously this man wanted to marry me and inseminate me immediately thereafter. Why else would a stupid computer game be so important? He loved me in a place where there's no cyber space or time. So Scrabulous became our new thing. We made dates to play—*Okay, be at your computer in an hour*—and our daily conversations were peppered with talk of word scores and numbered tiles. And then, of course, he screwed it all up again.

"I just don't want you to hold out for me," he said out of the total blue one day while we were spending quality time online. I'd mentioned a blind date I was maybe going on—maybe. He had to know I had options. Endless tiles!

"I see," I said from my couch.

"I dunno . . . ," he said from his. "I just don't want you to drop perfect guy for not-so-perfect me." My exhausted fingertips rested against the keyboard, and I watched our latest reconciliation disappear as he typed each new hurtful line.

"So I guess you're right," I wrote. "I'll move on."

"Geez Louise."

"What? That's obviously what you're saying." I was too exhausted to do anything but play the game. "Anyways, what does 'swap tiles' mean?"

"You lose your turn, but you can exchange your letters for new ones."

"K." Just perfect.

HELENA ANDREWS HAS THE BEST PUSSY IN THE WORLD

ABORTION MONKEY? Who wouldn't open that e-mail?

It was the winter of 2004, and my virtual load of junk mail was engorged to the point of needing medical attention. While sifting through spam from Seymour Butts and Mike Hunt to make sure nothing nonpervy got lost in translation, I noticed the most random coupling of nouns capitalized. Abortion and monkey. Not *tits* and *ass* or *pleasure* and *her* or *lottery* and *winner*, but *abortion* and *monkey* in all fucking caps. There was also the subject line to consider—"chimp." My inner pervert had been piqued.

"No wonder your father left you and that dyke," it read. Wait, what? Was this a telepathic telemarketer? Was I the unlucky member of a new golden demographic? And if so, what exactly was Abortion Monkey hocking—therapy?

The e-mail address didn't help any: helenaisastankape@hotmail
.com. At first it looked like Helenaisastan kape. Never been
there. Or maybe Helena I. Sastankape. Don't know her either.
Suddenly settling like a snow globe, I saw it for what it really
was—*Helena is a stank ape*. The fuck?

There was only one person in the history of the universe who
hated me so much that he'd take time out of his busy schedule of
being fucking nuts to come up with a clever alter ego and then
set said phantom up with its own e-mail account. Abortion
Monkey was his nom de guerre. First name Abortion, last name
Monkey.

This was microwaveable abuse. He knew that word would
fry my insides. Abortion, abortion, abortion, abortion. No matter
how many times I tried to make it toothless, it still gnawed. Had
anyone glanced over my shoulder to see it written in all caps?
Had they then cracked the code that was "helenaisastankape,"
and finally, like Occam, arrived to the so obvious conclusion that
at nineteen, with barely a peace sign's worth of sex partners, I'd
had an abortion using the money I got from my student health
insurance?

It happened sophomore year, right before falling in love for
the first time with Darin (hotmail known as Abortion Monkey).

◇◇◇◇◇◇

I've never wanted a Valium more in my entire life, but I still said no.

"Are you sure? Lots of women think they won't need it but
then find that the pill . . . eases their nerves. It can actually help
a lot." This was my preabortion "counselor" talking. A slender
black girl who I guessed was around my age and who had a boyfriend with whom she practiced "safer" sex. She went through

the steps of a too-long speech rehearsed more than once that day. It was 11:00 a.m.

Grant, my potential baby's daddy, had given me $200 the night before, unaware that Columbia's health insurance plan paid for "terminations." I figured he owed me, having acted like an asshole when I screamed in his face, "I'm fucking pregnant, you idiot." We were at a party on campus. Grant had spent the week prior trying to compel me into menses—"It's probably just stress." We had sex once, the fourth time I'd done it ever, and the condom broke (a phenomenon that seems to occur most prominently in the young and the retarded). The plan was for me to get the morning-after pill from Women's Health the next morning and for us to go back to being teenagers.

To Grant's credit, he felt guilty enough to endure the walk of shame with me. On the way back to my room, I tried holding his hand while he succeeded in avoiding mine. Once in front of McBain Hall, we gave each other a series of awkward friend pats and blended in with everyone else like nothing had happened or was happening.

There was a football game that day. I showed up at Health Services in my cheerleading uniform, standing in line behind a guy whose penis was apparently on fire. The whole setup was either ill advised or thought up by a devotee of Opus Dei. A woman whose sole job it was to make sure idiot kids didn't kill themselves over the weekend, known professionally as a triage nurse, sat behind a type of bank teller booth–slash–confessional in the middle of the waiting area. She was irritable and old, so mumbling your midnight transgression wasn't an option. A lot of stage whispering was going on. And because there were so many of us sinners, a line had formed, giving each of us a chance to mortify ourselves in public. I was on deck after the chick with vaginal itch. She got as far as "but there isn't any discharge or odor" when I left. *Pregnant? Me? Noooooo.*

Two weeks later, I sat corrected in that same building. I was too scared to purchase a pregnancy test from the neighborhood Duane Reade. Peeing in a cup and coming back for the results would be more private.

"So, according to this you're about three weeks pregnant," said a closeted gay man with a skinny tie and khaki pants.

"Really?" I asked, straining my neck to get a better look at whatever official papers he was getting his information from and hoping that maybe he'd read someone else's file by mistake, the file of some slutastic idiot who didn't know how to use a condom or self-restraint.

"Yep. Definitely. Pregnant. So, whoever the father is, now we'll see if he's really a real man." I had absolutely no clue what he meant by this, except maybe to say that Grant's masculinity was predicated on his reaction to the news, which was something like, "So I guess I have to pay for an abortion now?"

Weeks later, I tucked the stack of twenties he gave me in a pillowcase and rode the train alone to the P-Squared in Greenwich Village, because I supported their mission and figured no one would find me there, not that anyone was looking. My roommate, Stella, wanted to come with, but this wasn't a fucking shopping spree. Plus, I couldn't look at anyone looking at me like I was broken, ruined, condemned, or whatever. One soundless and snotty cry in the women's bathroom was all that was allowed. All that I could take.

I should have taken the Valium.

"I'm not nervous," I said, interrupting my counselor's soliloquy while folding in half one of the brochures she'd handed me about the "procedure" and what to expect when you want to stop expecting—touching the two edges together, then pinching the fat bulge in the middle and smoothing it down from one end to the other until it was perfectly flat. It's funny, the tiny bullshit things we remember when our lives are forever changing. "I'm just anxious."

A "technician" upstairs had the sadistic task of giving me an ultrasound. She told me the baby was five weeks old, or more mercifully, that I was five weeks along: still, I wished her a violent death. Up until then I'd been hoping this was all a terrible mixup or a practical joke orchestrated by the same zealots who do those "hell houses," where instead of a vampire jumping out a coffin, they've got a blond cheerleader getting a bloody abortion.

Just as gruesome were the hospital gown and vacuum hose I got. Whatever medieval torture techniques I'd previously imagined, it definitely wasn't that, but it was close. I also thought maybe they'd roll me into a white room with talking bunny rabbits and caterpillars and a magical blue pill that read "EAT ME" in cursive, which upon swallowing would make whatever was inside me grow smaller and smaller and smaller until it ceased to exist. Simple. Instead, two masked men debated for five minutes over whether or not they'd "gotten everything" with the Hoover attachment they had shoved into my womb, a part of my anatomy that I hadn't given much thought until that day. Numbed below the waist, I laid there for what seemed like forever, feeling like I'd been abducted. Finally a woman with a white coat walked in, reminded them there was "a patient on the table," and everything was taken care of.

No, I didn't have someone waiting for me down in the lobby. It was just me. No, nobody was going to pick me up. It was just me. No, I didn't need to call anyone. It was just me.

Changing back into my clothes, I felt fixed, glad to even be able to say "just me." What kind of monster was I? According to the unfolded pamphlet in my purse, a normal one. I checked to make sure I wasn't some horrible baby-killing fiend who danced naked on the tiny graves of the unborn at full moon. "You may have a wide range of feelings after your abortion. Most women ultimately feel relief after an abortion," it said under the heading "Your Feelings. . . ." I wished there was a less opinionated word for whatever had just happened to me, but I was happy for the second to my emotion.

I walked the long way back to the train station and caught a glimpse of myself in a storefront window. Hair? A little mussed. Nose? Normal. Lips? A bit dry and, in the middle, cracked. Teeth? Crooked on the bottom row. Cheeks? The same. Chin? Fat. Eyes? This game was stupid. There were flowers waiting for me on my extra-long twin. Stella. I fell asleep with plastic-wrapped carnations cradled in my arms.

◇◇◇◇◇◇

I told Darin, my soon-to-be first stalker, all of this not too long after he first said he loved me. He needed to know what he was getting. "I could have a fucking kid right now," I said, waiting for his disgust. "Lots of people could have kids right now," he said, wrapping his arms even tighter around my shoulders and shushing me to sleep. Right before winter break he gave me a card that read on the front, "All I want for Christmas," and then on the inside, "is YOU!" with a pop-up finger pointing straight at me.

So, the beginning of us was mostly just him promising me that I wasn't going to hell. When I broke it off two years later because I was twenty-one and that's what twenty-one-year-olds do, he made a decent living trying to send me there personally. A different finger was getting some exercise now. Darin was known on campus for being sort of militant—he was the strongest man pound for pound on the wrestling team and wore the same dark jeans and black Nikes every day unless I begged him to change—but aggressive love is what I needed then. Then when I didn't, he got on the offensive.

There were the random Darin sightings outside my dorm, because this was supposedly the quickest way to New Jersey, where he worked; the time he showed up at a party I was throwing with a "friend" he just couldn't seem to find, but since he was "already here, why not let's talk about us"; the spitting incident, which he later claimed wasn't all that bad, because the loogie landed near me, not *on* me; then the "accidental" tour down a flight of stairs, courtesy of his open palm to my back, and finally the trip to the police station.

"Yeaaaah," I said looking around the "precinct," thinking how much it resembled a public elementary school front office. "I think I need to get a restraining order." I was there on my lunch break.

"No problem, ma'am. Let's go sit down over there," said the black lady with lacquered nails and freeze-dried hair, pointing to a long metal table that would have been just as at home in an OR. We sat down to gossip. She typed while I talked. Turns out I had to file a "domestic violence incident report," which made me want to forget the whole thing. I wasn't a battered woman, just a bitter one. When your love life belongs to Dolly Parton's discography, you know it's time to switch gears. That's what I thought I had been doing when Abortion Monkey showed up, throwing bananas in my tail pipe.

It's hilarious that after all this time some people still seem to think themselves much more important than they truly are. I'm positive you've been waiting for me to send you a reply to this ridiculous e-mail all day long and I have never been one to disappoint.

Understand that I am in a place right now where your silly messages mean nothing to me. Continue to send them or don't, I could not possibly care any less.

It's interesting how when someone finds love, makes a great career move and is going somewhere purely positive in life someone else feels the need to drag them down (most likely from a complete lack of positivity in their own lives).

Darin, please get a life because mine has absolutely no room for you. . . . Helena

That would show his crazy ass. I raised my index finger high above my head, slamming it down on the send button with all the force of a carnival sledgehammer. Take that, monkey ass! I wanted to show him how much better at life I was. As evidenced in the line, "I could not possibly care any less," because so many "smart" people say "could care less," which implies that there is a rock bottom of caring that you have yet to strike, thus and therefore you do, in fact, care—most likely the exact opposite of what you were trying to say in the first place. Proper syntax was empowering when dealing with the man who once argued loudly that the correct phrase was not "get the gist" but "get the just." And that diarrhea was when you drank too much water and constipation was from not drinking enough. The e-mails kept coming:

FROM: Abortion Monkey
TO: Helena Andrews

SUBJECT: Re: Mighty Joe Young

Just hoping you're not still walking around with spit in your face, LMAO. By the way, congratulations on you and your new fag, I mean boyfriend.

We went for one more round. Me, spending an entire day crafting, spell-checking, editing, grammar-checking, revising, workshopping, and then copying and pasting the only two hundred words in the world capable of cutting him down a notch. Him, shutting me down with just two—Abortion Monkey. No matter how much high ground went into my e-sermon, once Darin hit his reply button—"Don't worry about responses, since I'll just delete anything else you send before reading it. Have a nice life, Mighty Joe Young!"—I'd get yanked from my pulpit, forced to lay my cursor hand on those two abject and filthy words. I was scared of them, felt sorry for them, and refused to delete them. I started solely referring to Darin as "the devil," hoping that he was, in fact, a liar.

Involving Frances in all this was out of the question—obviously. I'd handle Darin on my own, like always. Like the whole abortion situation. I refused to tell her then, because I knew she'd want to pray to father/mother God through the phone or make me wave a bushel of burning sage over my broken body. I couldn't take being taken care of. When I first started having sex, we had an ad lib conversation about penises and vaginas. *Where have you been, little brown-eyed girl?* Downstairs. *With who, that new boy?* Yep. *What kind of birth control are you two using?* Ma! *The sponge, the condoms, dental dams?* The pill! *Good.* She said if I got pregnant she wouldn't be angry—"Just send the baby down for me to raise until you finish school." Obviously, I'd decided not to take her at her word. In the process of becoming childless, I'd grown into a motherless child—untethered—not knowing my mother felt the same about herself once.

◇◇◇◇◇◇

Two days after graduation, we were on the floor of my first real apartment, leaning on old couch cushions Frances found somewhere on or around 125th Street in Harlem. She does these things, setting out on her own in the morning ("I'm just gonna go around the corner and see what's going on") and coming back hours later with somebody's trash and no man's treasure. I heard her in the stairwell before opening the door to see what she'd brought back now.

"Jesus friggin' Christ, woman! That's out on the corner for a reason, you know," I nagged, one hand on my hips and the other already reaching for my "new" toaster, futon frame, computer keyboard, or TV stand–slash–dinner tray–slash–"extra seating!" This time she was dragging three large sofa cushions in free clinic gray.

"Whaaa? You guys *need* this stuff," she answered, pulling her prizes into the hallway. I remembered how much I used to love her finding me funny-shaped sticks and seashells on the beach as a child, making me believe the ocean built all these things only for me. She lifted from the earth like a klepto—a bone-white stone, a retired snakeskin—and placed everything in my tiny accomplice's hands. For me? *Yes, sweet the beat, for you.*

The gray cushions would become our very own doctor's couch. With my new roommates gone and the thrill of graduation long gone, she started a serious talk about my so-called life, seeing as how the day before I burst into tears during the gospel song "I Feel Like Going On." The woman sitting next to us on the church pew handed Frances tissues that she passed on to me without a word. I hate church, and she knows it. She'd guilted me into going to the storefront chapel on the corner only because that Sunday had been Mother's Day. Funny.

Late the next day, we leaned on those old cushions, and I told her all about what I'd been up against. "There should be some kind of summer camp," I said, "because this business of being tossed out on our asses into the real world is shitty." Darin had just recently pushed me down a flight of stairs because he loved me and wanted to get back together. I didn't have a job with which to float my $550 share of the rent. The dark blue folder Dean Whomever handed me at the end of the graduation stage was empty because we owed Columbia more than a thousand bucks. And then there was the issue of the toddler that should have been cheering me on with the rest of the family.

"They told me to get rid of you, you know?" she whispered, sitting on the floor next to me, not looking at me. I was having growing pains, and she wanted to show me some of her own stretch marks, I guess. "But I didn't want to do that again."

It was 1972, and Frances was a pregnant sophomore in college. The story sounded so familiar, I wanted to stop her before she got started. *Wait a minute; we've seen this one already. Do a quick channel check.* She was the exact same age I'd been. In the middle of our mother-daughter bonding session, I learned we almost weren't mother and daughter.

She'd been in and out of love with my father Billy since high school, as well as a few girls she'd met at Humboldt State. She told me she'd gotten pregnant at nineteen and waited until the last legal minute to end it. Billy, who was in the navy, wanted to get married. He had it all planned out, she said. Frances would move back to Los Angeles—in with his mother—and wait for him to come back from long tours on a boat filled with men. She thought this idea ridiculous.

"Wendy said, 'Okay, Frances, if you're going to do this you have to do it now,' " she recalled my godmother telling her while her belly was getting bigger and she was still a teenager. The two drove up to San Francisco and got everything "handled." All I could think about was the scene in *Dirty Dancing* when Penny gets a botched abortion that no one really talks about aside from Baby's dad calling whatever "doctor" Penny went to a "butcher." I wonder whether Frances went to one of these dirty-wire-hanger-type places and whether whatever I did was any better.

My father was told after. So when Frances realized I was trying to exist in 1980, she wanted me—badly—and he was . . . blasé.

It might make other people feel, I don't know, *uncomfortable* to find out that they could have been aborted. That they could very well not be alive—conscious, in existence, present, or what-ever right at this moment—as they think, process, and type. Not me. Well, not me, really. I was chosen. Cho-sen. Didn't that count for more? Or maybe I'd been waiting in the wings since 1972, made invisible by a magical blue pill.

She told me that my grandmother and aunts, the majority of whom had found themselves pregnant before their eighteenth birthdays, sat her down to explain ever so calmly that babies weren't in her future.

"You can't bring a child around all that," my mother recalled them saying. All that, I'm guessing, meant freaky sex orgies— which most everyone can agree aren't childproof. I picture her mutinous then, defending her right to get knocked up just like everybody else. By then she was the only one of her seven sib-lings without a child and quickly approaching thirty (which is like forty when you adjust for inflation since 1980). I'm also guessing the grandchildren quota must have already been reached, or at least the grandchildren-from-lesbians-with-armpit-hair quota, which was obviously zero.

As a kid, I thought cameras and camcorders had not been invented before I turned five, because there does not exist any physical evidence of my being born. When I told her this, she laughed. *You didn't start the world, Raggedy Ann.*

It's really because my mother pretty much did the whole thing by herself.

For my last twenty-seven birthdays, we've had only one constant tradition—she must tell me the story of my birth. When I was smaller than her, I'd climb into her bed during the dark part of the morning and spread myself across her stomach, staring at her hard until she opened her eyes. Then I'd yell, "Tell me about when I was born!" She'd pretend not to hear me, squinting in my direction, staring at me through her eyelashes. I'd flail about my arms and legs as if drowning in her mommy tummy. "Tell me, woman!"

"Okay, okay, sweet the beat. Don't you get tired of hearing this?" she'd ask, already knowing the answer. "Every year it's 'Tell me about when I was born, tell me about when I was born.' " She sounded annoyed, but I knew she wasn't. Just the opposite. Who else would she tell her war stories to?

Frances was alone when her labor pains started. She took a cab to the hospital, where my grandmother worked as a nurse. "When I got there, everybody kept whispering, 'Oh, that's Effie's daughter.' So she knew I was there," my mother remembered in a sleepy voice. Then of course came all the horrible pushing and screaming. "My eyes turned blood red because I was holding my breath the whole time. The doctor kept yelling, 'Which way do you want her to come out?' "

I returned to her at 6:52 p.m. on October 28, 1980, three weeks late. She wanted a Libra—masculine, extroverted, and positive—so she started power walking in the hope that gravity would shake me awake and out. I missed the planetary alignment by five days and became a Scorpio instead—introverted, feminine, and negative. But somehow she still managed to love me.

We went over all this on my new couch cushions like high school best friends catching up at a reunion, surprised by how much they still had in common after so long, and sad about all the stuff that had changed. Frances wanted to know why I hadn't called to tell her about me and Grant. I told her I was fine.

"And what were you doing having unprotected sex, Lena?" my mother asked, singing the two syllables of my nickname to the tune of disappointment. Then I remembered why I hadn't called.

◇◇◇◇◇◇

I learned how to spell "sex" when I was six.

We were living with my mother's lover at the time, Mahasin, and her son Hamed, my "brother." They dressed us in matching corduroy overall shorts; mine were red and Hamed's, blue. At night we pulled them off and rubbed our tiny little kid bodies together while our mothers slept.

"Wanna know how to spell it?" Hamed asked one day without being prompted.

"Yes!" Of course I wanted to know how to spell it.

"S-E-X," he hissed slowly, leaning over to deliver the top-secret message directly into my ear, his lips brushing up against the tiny hairs on my lobe. Frances had informed us more than once that sex was a "grown-up game." This was subsequent to her catching us in the back of her old Chevy pickup truck in our underwear. I was on top. Immediately afterward, they sat us down and said that what adults did was different from what kids could do. So no more hanky-panky, just GI Joes and Barbies from now on.

"They're just mad," Hamed explained to me later, "because we do it the right way."

There was a wrong way? I figured it had to do with the fact that the two of us were a boy and girl, and our mothers, of course, were two girls. But I can't remember seeing Frances and Mahasin so much as kiss, let alone do *it* or anything. They shared a room down the hall, true. And they took showers and baths together. But then again, so did Hamed and me. I'd seen him naked tons of times, which was fine, because we were related—sort of. There didn't seem to be any difference in rightness between what they did and what the two of us wanted to do all the time. We'd sneak behind trees, under beds, in closets, and around corners just to hug each other really, really tight.

Eventually Frances and I moved away like we always did, and I'd forget I ever had a brother to squeeze the life out of whenever I needed. What stayed with me was the power that came from knowing how to write "sex," as well as the panic that I'd never be able to do it "the right way."

When I was fourteen, Vernell told me I should definitely try sex before marriage. "What if you didn't like it?" she asked, halfway explaining what frigidity was. *Or what if you simply didn't like penises? You wouldn't buy a car without a test drive, right?* I found her advice totally idiotic and irresponsible. Who says that to a teenager who just a few days before thought her vaginal discharge was a side effect of having contracted AIDS, her immune system secreting white blood cells? I shifted butt cheeks in my seat and rolled down the window, watching my childhood fade into the background with each passing palm tree. That's probably why I was so dead set against "losing it" in high school. I was already an A student starring in *Arsenic and Old Lace* between half-time performances; my rebellion was no rebellion. If everybody's doing it, then what the hell did they need me for?

Flash-forward a few years to New York City, freshman year, a single in John Jay, and my misplaced virginity—my disobedience shriveled. His name was Gary. He wasn't my boyfriend or anything, and we weren't dating. He'd just show up at JJ 602 after midnight, and I'd let him in because I didn't have anything better to do. The condom broke the third time we did it, and afterward he grilled me about the last time I'd had my period. I agreed to get the morning-after pill the next day and did. A year later I fell for his best friend, a guy named Grant.

◇◇◇◇◇◇

"And who was he?" Frances asked from the seat cushion next to mine.

"Just some guy," I said, realizing just how nonchalant all this sounded.

"Well, you know, I talked to Darin," she said, only alluding to his pushing me down some stairs.

"Jesus, woman, give it a rest. He's a fucking nut bag."

"I told him, 'You know, Darin, you can't be putting your hands on my daughter,' and he said, 'I know, Ms. Andrews. I know.' And you know what, he's really sorry, Lena. He loves you. He really loves you, and you should have someone here, close, that cares about you."

"Fine." This didn't shock me. She was ditching me three thousand miles away from home and wanted to make sure I had a ride back if need be. Darin had weaseled his way back into her good graces with promises of looking out for me and "never doing anything like that again, I swear."

"I'm serious," she said in a tone reserved only for occasions like this one—the "I'm Leaving on a Jet Plane" moment.

"I know. We'll see."

◇◇◇◇◇◇

A week later, I let Darin take me out to a fried chicken dinner. If Frances was right and he really did love me, then he'd be fine with helping me screw in my new venetian blinds—nothing else. I told him this much, and he bowed down to the table as if to tell a secret. "That's not what your mom said," he sang with an uptick to one side of his lip. Crooked.

Before she left, according to Darin, Frances told him that "the love stuff would come later," and that he should just hang in there until I came back around. I didn't have the heart to tell him the truth—that my mother just wanted me to be settled, ignoring the fact that I'd be settling. Hippie dyke revolutionary Peace Corps truants still don't know shit about free love or independence. Ironic, huh?

It didn't take long for Darin to go back to the "dark side." His. Words. In the time it took to put up my blinds, put together my futon, and then put to rest any hopes he had of our impending nuptials, he was back to threatening to kick my ass and explaining that he was only acting like this because we weren't together. One of my sorority sisters, Adrienne, offered up her dad and his steel bat. I said I was fine, grabbed my purse, and headed down to the precinct to spend lunch with the rest of the criminals and their victims, not sure anymore about which side I was on.

FROM: Helena Andrews
  TO: Abortion Monkey
SUBJECT: Re: Re: Mighty Joe Young

Darin,
It is clear that you have very serious mental/anger management issues that need to be resolved in order to become a functioning member of society. I have forwarded the

following e-mail along with your previous message to the New York City Police Department, which has both a Domestic Incident Report and previous warrant for your arrest already on file. I truly hope someday you learn to be a sane human being, instead of a violent and obsessive loon.

I signed my full name at the bottom and created a file folder entitled "Psycho Darin" for all Abortion Monkey's e-mails. Unable to delete them or look at them every ten minutes when checking my in-box, I told myself I was saving them for when I turned up missing.

It'd been more than three years since the e-mails stopped when the calls started.

"Hello?"

Nothing but static, not even heavy breathing of the pervert variety.

"Heeell-looo-ooo?" I knew someone was on the other end of that line, and despite evidence to the contrary, I wanted that person to admit it to me and to him- or herself.

"HELLO!" I'd yell after waiting another five minutes or more for whomever to say whatever it was he obviously needed to say at two o'clock in the morning.

The number was always "unknown," tricking me every time into picking up, thinking someone extremely classified was calling to whisk me away to the private island where all the awesome people live unencumbered by random phone calls in the night. "Number Unknown" would ring ten times in a row and then not at all for weeks. I knew it was Darin and wanted to be proved wrong.

"Hello?"

Silence.

"Darin, I know this is you, you effin' psychotic shit bag. Get a fucking life or eat a dick, either way stop calling me, you retarded monkey. How'd you even get this goddamned number? Are you STILL thinking about me every waking minute of your pathetic shit-stained life? I'm serious. Kick rocks!" A boulder-size lump had been forming in my throat the entire time I was talking, but I managed to get through the speech I'd saved up.

Silence.

"Ohmigod, listen, you fa—"

"Nineteen-oh-two Ninth Street Northwest," he was cackling. Hadn't heard his voice in years, but I knew. "Nineteen-oh-two Ninth Street Northwest. Nineteen-oh-two Ninth Street Northwest. Nineteen-oh-two Ninth Street Northwest. Nineteen-oh-two Ninth Street Nor—"

That boulder in my throat passed like a kidney stone, and I hung up before it got worse. How the hell did he know my address in Washington? I karate-chopped the front curtains and peered out at the empty street for a ninja second. There was no Darin standing on the sidewalk with a cell phone in one hand and a sickle in the other. I was safe—for now. This time, though, I called my mother.

First, she apologized for entertaining the possibility of Darin and me being friends so many years ago. "I'm so sorry I didn't listen to you from the beginning, little brown-eyed girl," she said in one sigh, a faraway lilt in her voice.

"I know, Ma." I figured she was somewhere back in the '60s in a house where a violent man ruled absolutely and her "in case of emergency" task was to grab her younger sister, leap out a window, and head down the street to her grandmother's, the safe house. "I know," I said again.

Turns out it was all MySpace's fault. I'd written a blog about ex-boyfriends, not naming names, of course, but Darin must have read the part about "crazy-psycho-stalker-jerk face" and recognized his. Naturally, this was reason enough for him to begin a campaign against me. Frances, who'd gotten all this information from Darin's mom, was upset with me.

"Why are you writing about Darin anyway? You need to set all your stuff on these sites to private, Lena. You never know who's reading it."

"Fine," I said.

"I'm serious," she said.

What I didn't tell her was that I wasn't the only person on Abortion Monkey's phone list. My "boyfriend" at the time, a Muslim podiatrist named Abdul, was shocked to hear the whole Darin story, which had been abridged over Duccini's and Netflix.

"So yeah, I'm staying off MySpace for a while, laying low like *I* did something."

"You know what? Now that you mention it, I think I did get a call from dude not too long ago," said Abdul without alarm, as if getting a call from a mental patient was normal.

"Umm, what?"

"Yeah. I thought it was weird. Some guy called me. He was like, 'Hello, this is—' "

"Darin? Did he say his name was Darin?"

"I can't remember what he said his name was. But he was like, 'Yeah, hello, this is such and such, and I just wanna let you know that Helena Andrews has the best pussy in the world.' Then he hung up."

If I hadn't already fainted once that year, I would have blacked out from sheer exhaustion like the celebrities do. I didn't know whether to take it as a compliment or curse. I was doing it, sure, but what I really wanted was to find *it* (love, longevity, the meaning of life), and here I was wasting time with a podiatrist on depression meds who'd told me no less than three times that "this wasn't a relationship." What *this* was, only he knew, and he wasn't telling.

Darin, on the other hand, was an oversharer. The best pussy in the world? Try the pussy of least resistance.

WALK LIKE A WOMAN

It has been suggested more than once that I have some type of problem.

"If you're consciously choosing to do something to the obvious exclusion of your own personal safety, then something's clearly wrong. You need to go to meetings where people sit on folding chairs. Take a friggin' cab!" commanded a concerned friend through my cell phone as I strolled down a dodgy D.C. street, the sun setting on my back. Me not giving a damn about maybe getting mugged for the third time or fainting for the second.

That's my issue: I walk too much.

In the face of my driver's license deficiency and an abhorrence for the close body contact prevalent on most metro systems, I've learned through pluck and circumstance to use the legs God gave me. People, I've walked across state lines—multiple times— without getting winded or wreathed. Never thinking twice about the damage being caused to the thinning skin above my smallest three toes until it was too late, I average five, maybe even six, miles a day without even trying. Pedometers are for pussies.

When I stop to think about it, which one tends to do a lot of on foot, like all my potentially damning idiosyncrasies the walking is a product of my childhood and therefore can easily be blamed on my mother. Forcing me to "go outside and play," Frances inadvertently created a pedestrian. On Catalina, where I was an only child with tons of friends but fewer equals, spending time alone was habitual and safe. Why walk all the way across the street to ask if Melissa and Marcy could come out and play when there was an unguarded pomegranate tree just a forty-minute mile from here?

I'd march about for hours, my skinny grade-school gams working like a windup toy possessed, trying to get lost in a town the size of a liberal arts college campus and feeling secure in knowing that was impossible. We lived on an island. Nobody got lost, no matter how many times they went fishing drunk.

Besides, the more time I spent with myself, the more I liked it—or me, rather. Imaginary friends: who needs 'em? Plus, there was a lot of stuff on my mind, stuff I would've never known about if me, myself, and I hadn't begun our long jaunts across the beach, our hikes up beer-bottled hills, and our parades downtown. Like the fact that Justin Ramirez could scarcely contain his passion for me, which is why he'd ignored me during *The Pirates of Penzance* rehearsal. And Amy Dugger's dad hadn't "forgotten" to pick me up for the camping trip on the Isthmus. And getting traded in the middle of the Little League season was not, as Frances would have me believe, the price of being too talented.

I'd come back inside by the time the would-be streetlights came on (on Catalina there was no use for them), feeling rather productive and not at all as if I'd spent five hours wandering aimlessly while conducting an existential conversation with myself. Frances would inevitably ask, "What you been up to, little brown-eyed girl?" And I'd answer truthfully, "Nothing much. Just walking." The interview ended there, and we'd begin our Vaudeville dinner theater. Act 1, scene 1:

"Heeey, good looking. Whaaat-cha got cooking," I'd sing, two-stepping my way through the narrow hallway that moonlit as our kitchen.

"Dooo you wanna shimmy with meee? I said, dooo you wanna shimmy with meee," Frances chanted back.

"No time for dancing, I wanna eat! What's for dinner, woman?"

She'd holler, "French-fried boogers and cocoa snot," which was always quite good.

By the time we moved off the island and to Los Angeles, twelve-year-old me thought singing for my dinner was dumb. I was disappointed in my mother's failure to provide two essentials: speech therapy and a student RTD pass. The city's Rapid Transit District buses were strained with the residue of society, a near-impossible clog to shift through with the surfer girl accent I'd picked up. "Omigah, is this me, brah? Du-u-ude, did I just miss my thingy?" Because nobody cared or understood enough to answer, inevitably I'd get off way before or way after my stop, booking it five city blocks to make it to "advanced" math class at Mt. Vernon Middle School. Its mystique vanished with the stress of being lost for real, walking, like college-ruled paper and sensible tennis shoes, had been ruined by necessity. Nobody walks in Los Angeles.

Imagine then what a relief New York was. An entire city filled with the sort of people able to perform the difficult task of getting from one place to the other without a care but with purpose. Talking to themselves along the way. Since everybody was crazy, nobody was crazy. This was me, this was home. Some days on Columbia's campus, there would be a sighting of this one Asian guy we called "crazy cell phone man." You heard him before you saw him. He'd be trying to earn Contemporary Civ. participation points by shouting into his palm: "You call that man's *in*humanity to man? What could be more human than suffering and pain? Who causes these things? Aliens?" If there was a cell phone somewhere in there, I never saw it. I followed him from behind once when we were going the same way down College Walk, noting the reactions of folks coming from the opposite direction. " . . . and if philosophers are to become kings, what then will kings become? Aliens?" Nobody gave him a second glance or even shared with me a knowing smirk—*"this* guy . . ." I kept straight after he turned toward the library, probably headed to the stacks to make sweet love to whoever was on the other side of that "phone," or maybe just his palm.

That's the thing that got me so turned on about walking in New York: nobody sees nothing. You could go miles down Amsterdam Avenue, surrounded on every side by papis looking for mamis, tourists looking for safety, worshippers looking for succor at St. John's, and addicts looking for the cover of Morningside Park—but never you. Getting lost in thought was easy when nobody was looking—or so I thought. Apparently, it's also easy to overlook everyone else. Word around campus was that Helena, that light-skinned pretty Delta, didn't know how to speak to anybody. Those in the know knew I needed glasses.

After graduation, I got an internship at *O, The Oprah Magazine* that paid $5 and some change an hour. Our offices were on Fifty-third on the west side, and I lived on East 128th Street. Making minimum wage also meant choosing between a monthly metro card and regular sustenance. Seeing as how I'd never get ahead with a loud stomach—*So, Helena, do you think you can fact-check October's contributors' page? GROWL!*—I chose the latter. What's a seventy-five-block trek twice a day between professionals?

In Washington three years later, I'd tell people this story as proof of payment for all these alleged "dues" people talk about. "Every fucking day, each way. One time in the rain with high-heeled boots and a two-dollar umbrella."

By then I had a master's degree *and* a metro card. Neither new development—supposed intelligence or cheap rides—stopped me from walking home after my shift at the *Times* ended around midnight. Yes, I had a shift, which in itself suggests back doors leading to alleys decorated with piss, cigarettes, and bonfires for bums. And also "breaks." People who have shifts should probably get to take breaks. But it seems that people who have degrees *and* shifts do not. Gallivanting around town on foot and after the freaks come out was my idea of a good break.

I was just getting a handle on the night shift when it happened. Tuesdays were my Fridays, and on Fridays I came in at four and then left around elevenish if nothing "broke." On one particular balmy Friday night (but not *my* Friday, which would've been Tuesday), I decided it was way too nice outside to be cooped up on the Green Line to Greenbelt and instead decided to walk from our offices on Sixteenth and I streets near the White House to my house on Ninth and T—about twenty-minutes away if I powered through. My usual route went first through Dupont, which I had deemed safe due to the high concentration of gays, and then on to U Street, which because of gentrification was also risk-free. Everything was going according to plan until I got to T and Tenth.

There's always a stretch of one's residential world that one considers either stupid or annoying. A chain-link fence messing up the order of wrought iron? Annoying. A wooden puppy hunched over in crapping position with "NO!" painted on its back? Stupid. In this case, on the well-lit Ninth Street, there was a stupid abandoned row house two doors down from my newly renovated basement, in front of which a bunch of annoying hooligans held a nightly game of concrete craps. Because walking through this foolishness meant no fewer than five hoots and three hollers, I'd decided months before that walking up the dimly lit and suburbanly silent T Street was the wiser choice.

Just a block away from home, I spotted two teenage boys walking at me. I got brief glimpses of them from under my umbrella. Oh, yeah, it'd started raining. They seemed harmless, although curiously alert given the hour. It was a little past midnight, and the tall one was rapping loudly down the pavement part of the street, while his partner provided the beats from the sidewalk. Too tired to switch sides, I made a note of them and kept it moving.

By the time we met in the middle of the block, our paths crossed without incident. They went their way and I continued on mine, already fingering the front door key in my coat pocket.

You know that feeling you get when someone is staring at you from behind? Evidence that there exists some type of spiritual kinetic energy between all human beings that we're just too primitive to tap into and use to stir coffee with our minds? About two seconds after avoiding whatever situation happens after dark between two men and a woman on a silent street, that feeling hit me like a fist to the face. Thankfully, they didn't use anything that dramatic.

"What the fuck?" They were on me in an instant, the tall one tugging on my purse before I had a chance to process the idea of being robbed. It was ridiculous. Who makes a decent living wage pickpocketing besides nineteenth-century British foundlings? Clearly this was not a mugging but this kid's scary attempt at flirting. *Sorry, homie, but I'm grown. Move along, please, I've got z's to catch.*

"Gimme the bag," he said, the growing size of his eyes conveying his seriousness. His rapping partner closed in on the left side, and I was boxed out with basketball-camp-for-inner-city-youth efficiency. This is also around the time I first contemplated screaming "FIRE!" which, according to the self-defense class Frances made me take as a twelve-year-old, is what you yell when someone's either trying to rape or murder you. Nobody wants to muddy up his or her house shoes running after a serial killer. But anybody will vault from naked Twister to watch a neighbor's nest egg go up in flames.

"No!" Now see, this objection flew from my lips totally without my knowledge. In fact none of my subsequent actions were preapproved—yanking my purse strap back onto my shoulder, parking my free hand onto my hip, and assuming what can only be described as a ninja stance. Despite being well aware of the fact that my life was worth more than an XOXO bag circa 1999, I literally couldn't help myself.

"Give. Me. The. Bag." I finally let go with all the petulance of a preschooler just learning to share. *Fine then! Here.* The shorter one, feeling neglected, kept himself busy with my pockets, patting them down and asking three times for "the cash." "Where's the cash? Is there cash?"

"There's no money in that bag, sir. Sir? Sir, there's nothing to be had in my pockets," I said, pleading in the most professional manner I could think of. Maybe I could appeal to their more genteel sides, or at least throw them off with my olde English and run in the other direction while they looked over their shoulders for whoever had on the top hat.

Then it was over. With my "leather" purse in hand and a fist full of lint, these two sixteen-year-old scalawags took off in the opposite direction like they stole something. With that simile forever ruined, I felt more disappointed than debased. *That was it?* Without a phone with which to call the authorities or my mother, I decided walking another block and a half to the metro wouldn't be tempting fate. Plus, it's not like I had anything left to lose. On the ride down the escalator, I kept looking around to see if people were staring—if I looked like someone who'd just been robbed by children.

I burst into tears only after asking the two officials behind the bulletproof glass if I could please use their official MTA telephone to call the police. One of the station agents, an older black man in a uniform hat, looked me in the eye and asked, "Oh, sweetheart, what's wrong?" It's a surprise they understood anything through all the stuttering and snot. "Someone-heehuh-just-heehuh-stole-heehuh-my-heehuh-purse-heehuh." The waterworks didn't stop until Adrienne drove up with a steel bat. "We gonna ride around till we find these fuckers."

A few days later, this white guy rang my doorbell, claiming to have found some things that belonged to me. Jumpy but newly armed with pepper spray, I stuck my free hand through the gate. In it he placed my address book, emptied wallet, *Wicked*, and a dog-eared copy of *The Sex Chronicles* that wasn't mine, I swear. Quickly closing the door and thanking him through the window, I figured life didn't suck so hard after all and immediately went back to my walking, which after the night in question provided an even bigger break from work, my head, my life, whatever. Pedestrian meditation was anything but. This time, however, there was the added bonus of it being banned, making my late-night rendezvous with myself all the more irresistible.

In time I had to lie about how I was getting home, since it was now everyone's job to make sure I didn't get murdered along the way.

"I'm just gonna go up to K Street," I fibbed, waving a bus away while waiting for the light to change. "It's easier to catch a cab from there."

"Fine. Call me when you get home," said whoever was assigned to me that night. A text an hour later was always good enough—"Goin 2 bed. Holler."

It was in the middle of another lie—telling Gina that I was waiting for the bus to go home and definitely not walking there—when I got cut short by a burning sensation in my right bicep.

"Aaaaaah!"

"Dude, what the fuck?" she asked from the other side of the phone.

"This asshole with dreadlocks just grabbed my bag. I can't believe this shit!"

"Dude, what?"

"He snatched. My effin'. Bag. From off. My effin'. Shoulder." I was starting to get winded.

"And where are you?"

"Running after his ass."

"What?"

"Don't play yourself, asshole! Don't. Play. Yourself!"

It was the 911 operator who convinced me to stop running. Something about her not being able to do anything for me over the phone if he decided to graduate from misdemeanant to felon. The police officer that showed up to my rescue grudgingly agreed to drive me home only after I admitted to having been robbed just three weeks earlier. He called it in as I slid into the backseat, feeling like a badass. "Copy that."

For obvious reasons, I was all too happy to get a real reporting job without hooker hours about six months thereafter. For equally obscure ones, I kept on walking, this time from our offices in the great state of Virginia through the popped polo collars of

Georgetown and the striped button-downs of Dupont, on to the furry hoodies of U Street, then on through the designer jeans of Little Ethiopia and finally into the bat cave. I firmly believed lightning doesn't strike thrice, or maybe I just couldn't let the terrorists win. Either way, the four-mile trek soon became something like an addiction. I say "like" because admitting you have a problem is the first step on the road to recovery, and that was the one direction I wasn't headed.

It was a headache that scared me straight.

The weather in Washington is something akin to a "domesticated" lion let loose in the wild after years of drinking from a toilet—unpredictable. On this particular morning, it was freezing outside, so I wore a huge black puffy coat to work. But by the time I left that evening to start my hour-long walk home, the temperature had shot up to hot as balls. Unfazed by this, I strapped my twenty-pound laptop to my back and said my goodbyes. About twenty minutes in I sensed something might be wrong when I felt something warm and wet run down my thighs. I bent over for a second to peek between my legs to see if I'd had an "accident." Nope, just sweat. Lots and lots of sweat. Realizing then that I probably had a Rorschach inkblot of perspiration shaping up nicely on my ass and back, I decided leaving my coat on would be best. It would also be a fitting penance for not taking the metro, or the bus, or a cab, or a rickshaw.

Once I finally got home, I threw that fucking coat off like it was on fire, flinging it across the living room with one hand and freeing myself from my now-gazillion-pound laptop with the other. I've never been thirstier in my life. I downed three highballs of Brita in as many seconds and then headed for the door again. Thirsty *and* starving. My mouth watered for a personal pan pizza from Duccini's, about twelve blocks down the street. I could've had a larger pizza delivered, I could've taken the 90 bus straight down, I could've grown my own organic tomatoes on the windowsill and made a pizza using those and rat meat, but I didn't, okay—I walked.

By the time I got inside, the temperature in my head had to be at least 187 degrees Fahrenheit. There was a new girl taking the orders up front, which pissed me off because the African guy with the Mets cap always gave me a free Fanta. Two ten-year-olds in Catholic school uniforms played with dolls under the counter, and the brunette behind me got her order taken before mine. Pissed, I walked up to lean on the counter more than I should've been, my eyelids way heavier than they should've been. I had an epiphany about the word *throbbing* being an example of onomatopoeia, and everyone in there suddenly became stupid, fat, and ugly.

"Excuse me? Hello? Are you gonna take my order? Jesus." I couldn't friggin' believe how rude the new girl was being.

"I'm sorry; I didn't know you were ready." If she was shocked by my volume, she didn't let on.

"Obviously! An eight-inch pepperoni."

"No problem, ma'am. Let me just—"

"I mean, can I pay now? Jesus!" Why the hell was this chick so slow on the uptake? I looked around for some sympathy and came up with nothing but dirty looks.

"Right. Sure. That'll be five dollars."

Reaching into my coat pocket (yes, I put that coat back on) for my wallet actually felt like digging for clams. I took a tiny step back to steady myself, and then everything turned gray. The woman with the dark hair yelled, "No no no no," and I woke up on the fake linoleum.

Fainting is your body's inconvenient way of telling you to take a time-out. I had never fainted before and never want to faint again, despite having previously thought the act romantic and Elizabethan. The new girl was on the phone with 911 (me again), and the African guy was on his way with a cold Fanta. I told them I was fine, no really. Just a little hot and tired. I thanked the brunette for catching me and shooed her hand away when I got up off the floor. They charged me for the pizza. I ate it on a stool in the corner, holding each piece up to my mouth with one shaky hand and a grape Fanta to my head with the other. Pleading the fifth, I won't say how I got home.

Frances forbade me from walking for a month and made an appointment with my primary care physician, who one EKG and some blood work later said that I had been tired and hot.

For a while I was good—taking the metro to *and* from work, staying hydrated, carrying my pepper spray with the safety off, and ordering my pizza in. Really, I was just too embarrassed to show my face around town, seeing as how it had played me so tough. I'd been held up by teenagers, made bruised and bagless by someone else, and then collapsed in front of strangers and to-go boxes. Perhaps I should lay off the walking for a while, I thought, if only to trick Washington into believing I was gone. Then maybe whatever hoodoo had been placed on my hobby might get lifted—hopefully in time for the cherry blossoms.

I had to ease back onto the street, hopping off the train a few stations before I was supposed to or catching the bus a few blocks away. Duccini's was the last stop on my comeback tour.

It'd been a while, so I had a speech prepared. It began, "So, it turns out I'm not deranged, just a little dehydra . . ." Fortunately, I didn't need it. The African guy spotted me mumbling to myself outside and was shouting by the time I got my foot in the door. "Hey! My friend. I was worried about you."

DRY V-WEDGIES

I've got a bag of Adaoha's stuff going stale on the bottom shelf of my bookcase. Next to that is a bundle of unopened mail with her name on it. They've been there for a while now, since before and way after her funeral. I refuse to open either, much less make direct eye contact. I threw out bravery for such things with my Amy Grant tape and sadistic sleepover games.

Adaoha has become either Bloody Mary or the Tooth Fairy, depending on whether I miss or hate her. Some days she makes me afraid of my own reflection, and I have to sneak past the bathroom mirror to get in the shower, embarrassed and dirty. Afterward, with the room all misty, I squeegee only the skinniest slice of mirror with my right hand, wiping the shower sweat away with one swift karate move. Despite the badass technique, I'm still too scared to look for too long. Even the thirty seconds it takes to wash my face freak me out. Something could easily materialize behind my back while I'm bent over the sink with my eyes trapped shut by soap. Once I've straightened out, I still don't look.

◇◇◇◇◇◇

"Helena? Hey. Do you need a ride?" The voice on the other line was feathery soft, almost ephemeral, reminding me of a grade-school teacher's after a problem child has saturated his or her pants. More than an inside voice, this was a voice inside my head.

I happened to be taking a mental health day that afternoon. Too scared of what I might do with access to the Internet at work—continue refreshing certain people's Facebook pages and writing biting one-liner away messages—I'd decided to spend the day more sanely. As I furrowed into the farthest reaches of the bat cave better known as the bedroom of my basement apart-ment, the last thing I wanted to do was talk to anyone about anything unless it was a certain person named Dex begging for my forgetfulness. The calls kept coming.

None of them were him. Each time the phone rang, I'd wait a few rings before pulling it from my pillowcase. Three-oh-one. Somebody from Maryland. Ignore. That became impossible as the calls kept coming. Four in an hour. Fine, fine, I stopped feel-ing sorry for myself long enough to answer. It was a friend of Adaoha's and a club friend of mine at best; thus far our telecom-munication only involved the very occasional text. I must have forgotten something major—another Dirty Thirty birthday cele-bration, perhaps. Smooth. See what this dude was making me do? I was fucking up on my friends! I was missing out on a chance to scream, "Woo-hoo, you're old, bitch!" at a woman I didn't know but felt sorry for in a crowd of twenty-somethings too busy belting out Beyoncé lyrics to care that they were next. An excuse was worked out in my head by the time I reached into the pillow.

"Oh, uh, hey lady," I croaked, attempting to come off equal parts drunk, germ-infested, and sleepy. "What's going on? Am I supposed to be getting dressed?"

"What?" She sounded lost, possibly doubting my ability to go from zero to sexy in minutes.

"Seriously, I can put some clothes on in . . ." An outfit was worked out in my head by the time my feet hit the floor.

"No. Helena, you don't know?"

"What?" It was my turn to be skeptical.

"Adaoha died last night." And rip goes the Band-Aid.

Ignoring the invention of the perm, black chicks are not susceptible to magic. We don't go up in clouds of smoke. We don't disappear down suspect rabbit holes. We don't walk into coat closets, never to be heard from again. Plans have to be made, hair has to be pressed, and bags of stuff have to be packed.

Black chicks don't do this. They aren't supposed to just up and leave, because they have expert knowledge about just how much that shit sucks. They know how much no one wants to be the asshole getting left. The one standing at the edge of responsibility, too tired to lie down and too reasonable to leap. The one on the receiving end of all those tears and snot and spit and shit and piss and blood and cum and whatever other carnal fluid nature makes a living getting rid of.

She got rid of us. I would do the same to her, except I have this bag of Adaoha that I'm actively ignoring right now. It's my new thing. Some days I pretend to forget it's there.

Those same nights, I think she might come for me in the middle and sneak something special under my pillow or maybe snatch me away to the place that only she knew about. Maybe she'll show me the secrets she kept there. Because this whole time, she had to have known something we didn't about whatever was on the other side of that fall that was so much fucking better than staying on solid ground with us.

I say "us" like we were a gang. Maybe we were, and jumping was the only way out.

◇◇◇◇◇◇

The girl was offering me a ride to Adaoha's parents' house in Maryland. We—the friends who knew her best—were gathering there to console and have council. What happened? Nobody knew, the girl said. She'd been found. Found. She'd done this to herself. Nobody mentioned the word that rhymes with civic pride. We don't even smoke cigarettes.

The girl's voice was still in my head, saying she figured I was ignoring her calls because I already knew. Because I didn't want to talk. I didn't. If I said another word, the feeling might come back to my tongue.

"No, that's okay," I said. "Adrienne will take me."

Fuck. Now I have to tell Adrienne. I call, and she doesn't pick up. I text something urgent. She calls back—was coming out of class. Law school. She is laughing with someone. I don't want to say it, don't want to change her. I almost hang up. Whoever's walking next to her is laughing like a maniac. There is the opposite of a pregnant pause. I contemplate hanging up again.

"Yeah, what's up," she said.

"Adaoha died last night," I say.

"What?"

In times of crisis, *what* gets the most use out of any of the five W's. Like *fuck*, it's ambidextrous, able to play both sides by way of inflection. *What* (emphasis on the "tuh") demands an answer. *Whaaaa* (with an endless "ah," almost like pi) is genuine shock and awe. *What* (with a breathless "whuh") is deflated, defeated.

We practiced each one over the next week, as if rehearsing for something thrown together at the last minute. Everything was hectic, and nothing was patient.

We'd become walking automated voice systems. No matter how hard you raged against the machine, "What" was the only response, when the obvious prompt should have been "Why"? We didn't bother to ask until six feet of packed dirt buried any hope of an answer. I probably didn't want to hear it anyway—I probably would have told Adaoha, *Keep it moving, please get it together, do something with yourself,* or something like that. Maybe I'd cursed her, killed her. On a church pew, guilty tears threatened my face, twisting it into something so grotesque I was terrified it might freeze that way forever if someone happened by and slapped me on the back.

Funerals fucking suck. The name itself brings to mind stiff organs, whorish makeup, and venereal disease (for me anyway). To remedy that in civilized circles, the ceremony is renamed a "homecoming," which itself brings to mind broken beer bottles, communal anger, and matching uniforms. The tailgate was in the bat cave. I went into overdraft buying a dozen white roses to make corsages out of and was blessed with a mindless two hours, wrapping green floral tape around freshly cut stems.

There is a false sense of accomplishment in numbers and costume. The corsages were for us—her sorority sisters. Standing in my kitchen, each of us pinned one above the heart of another, making sure it wasn't crooked. The actual ceremony was an ominous afterthought. It was all about the preparation, preparation, preparation. Which of course all went to shit as soon as we saw Adaoha in a coffin. A fucking coffin. Another word in desperate need of a euphemism.

The flowers had to be white. White like the dresses we wore when we became sisters. When Adrienne, LaKia, and I saved

Adaoha from a life sentence of nerd alerts. Despite the pats on the back we gave ourselves, she still turned out better than us. See, we all had the same bag. Note here that I am not speaking in the metaphorical sense, that each one of us tiny human beings has some tiny "bag" of fear and loathing festering on the bottom "shelf" of our "bookcases." No, I mean that Adaoha, Adrienne, LaKia, and I each have the same exact bag. We got them as presents on the night we were made Deltas. After a nationally sanctioned and predetermined period of learning about sisterhood, scholarship, and service—and also screaming, sit-ups, and sleep deprivation—we put on those white dresses, said a few magical words, and poof, we were related.

Adrienne I'd known since hating her freshman year. We lived in the same dorm, but not the same planet. It was me, her, this tall guy who played the saxophone like a virgin, and a girl who wore ankle-length jean skirts and Keds topped with tube socks. Those were the blacks on our floor. From a scientific point of view, I took an educated guess that all black people on campus were either geeks or militant (Adrienne wore loose-laced Timbs). I decided to hang out with white people and got hanged for it. Supposedly a mental memo went out to all the Black Student Organization members. I'd been Oreo listed.

I had no clue how bad it was until one drunken night in the elevator to the sixth floor. Hamish, who was Irish or British and smelled like chlorine and foot fungus, was seeing me home after too much "punch" from a house with Epsilon or Chi on the facade. Adrienne, her good friend LaKia, and a bunch of fellow conscious card-carrying black girls were coming from something with "African" or "Malcolm" on the flyer. Buried in Hamish's pasty neck, my arms wrapped around his concave swimmer's waist, I never heard what they were whispering about. But when we got out, I saw the looks—disgust, shame, envy maybe.

After that, Adrienne was just a fancy Bed, Bath and Beyond shower basket in the bathroom, overstuffed with Victoria's Secret lotions. We never spoke, but I had a speech prepared in case of an eminent showdown. It began thusly: "First of all, I'm from Compton. I have a cousin on death row. I went to public school for a friggin' entire year. You don't know my life!" And my ghetto résumé went on from there.

As fate would have it, though, my oratorical skills would go untested, because one shitty work-study job grilling hot dogs for outside "jams" later, the two of us were inseparable. Adrienne made me go to $3 pajama parties at the Pan African house, saving/drowning me in a mosh pit of black bodies pulsating to the xylophone stylings of "Money, Cash, Hoes."

One semester later and I was deemed sufficiently black enough for even the most discerning of palettes. I rebelled by letting Spencer Schulz, a blond Floridian of German descent, lick my fingers in private and hold my hand on College Walk. Hey, I enjoyed white people *and* delicious Korean BBQ. But the Benetton ads of my teens had been canceled. Welcome to the real world as experienced through four years of voluntary social segregation. Having seen *School Daze* on VHS, DVD, and BET, I figured joining up with somebody might help simplify things.

So, Delta. Adaoha thought all we had to do was sign our names on a sheet numbered one through five, and then al-lakhazam, we'd be in. "Umm, no, honey," was the thought bubble that hovered above every already-Delta. "Do your research." That meant going to all their parties, study breaks, and women's forums on the state of black relationships as depicted in *Love and Basketball*. Adrienne and I, having done the aforementioned research, knew all the tricks—have at least one intelligent thing to say per run-in with a sister, covet the color red but never think of wearing it, and always stay till the end.

Adaoha, we thought, didn't have a chance, seeing as how she was a total weirdo, one of those black folks on campus who do hang out with other black folks, but not the normal kind, so they might as well be hanging out with white people. That was me before Adrienne saved/drowned me with black lip liner and Lil' Kim. Adaoha should've gone first, maybe.

Somehow she made it in—something to do with a 3.6 GPA. So, it would be the five of us—me, my new best friend Adrienne, her friend LaKia, Adaoha, and her freak of a friend from the women's college across the street, Darienne. We all lived together temporarily while studying for the DAT—the Delta Aptitude Test, which every candidate for membership had to pass. Grudgingly, the five of us spent Spring Break '00 in my double in McBain Hall (Stella was gone on vacay). We figured the bigger the room, the less likely it'd be that anyone would have to breathe the same direct air as Darienne.

This is going to sound extremely elementary, but Darienne picked her boogers and then ate them, according to Adrienne, who knew her from nursery school or something. She could have been reformed, having completed the twelve-step program for chronic nose diggers better known as puberty, but we didn't give a shit about any of that. Adrienne said, we laughed, and Darienne was marked.

It didn't help that she still lacked the basic life skills of any human being not raised by benevolent wolves. Deodorant was exotic to her, as were hot combs and the plastic drugstore kind. Then, of course, there was the conspicuous snot mustache we couldn't rightly make fun of because she was scheduled for functional endoscopic sinus surgery somewhere in the distant future. Since medically diagnosed conditions are by definition unmockable—openly—we instead implied our resentment, hoping she'd infer her way to social betterment. Sometimes I felt sorry for her, but most times I just wished she'd wipe her fucking nose. Being her ace boon coon, Adaoha either didn't care, was too good to notice, or pretended not to, so it was up to Adrienne and me.

One 3:00 a.m., the five of us were delirious with facts about Delta's maternity ward in Africa when, predictably, the talk turned to our own vaginas. I thought this would be an A and B conversation with the only two nonvirgins (me and LaKia) hosting a smutty talk show for a captive audience of one (Adrienne). As usual Adaoha had her nose in a book, and Darienne . . . well, come on. But to our double surprise, Darienne had something to say about double happiness "up against the wall." "Oh, yeah, that's the best," she said, interrupting us with a nasally nonchalance we'd never heard before and would never believe.

She even went so far as to provide a visual aid, her mouth open and head thrown back to one side in mimed rapture and her arms thrown above that ridiculous scene, stopped short by an imagined wall of sin. Eyes. Wide. Shut. We could've just ignored her, as was our usual coping method, but it was dangerously past midnight, when boredom and ridicule become obvious bedfellows.

"With who?" someone asked, while the others feigned disinterest.

"A boy from my neighborhood," Darienne answered neatly, excited to be part of the conversation but still skeptical of whether she was in in.

"Your boyfriend?" someone else asked, without sounding too interested . . . or disgusted.

"Something like that." She was getting coy.

"Was iiit . . . good?"

The cross-examination continued until we veered off into really dangerous territory—early '90s R&B. Hypnotized by Darienne's tall tale of the phantom booty call, we forgot how much we hated her long enough to let her eavesdrop. Listening to us reminisce on the real love we had back in the summah, summah, summah time of our youth, we thought maybe she'd learn a thing or two about how we do it. As luck would have it, SWV's jam "Weak" was everybody's favorite. Adaoha, studying, ignored us. Kia, the silent but deadly type, let another one rip from far enough away that it seemed innocent. "Remember the Butterfly?" she asked, talking to us but looking at Darienne. We surrounded her like professionals.

"Hell, yeah," I said, skywriting the familiar figure eight with my kneecaps—a dance move that took me three PE's to learn in middle school.

"Thanks, Debbie Allen. It's like this," sang Adrienne, mimicking me and mocking what we all knew Darienne could never do. These were the pelvises of cool kids. Kids who knew when to wipe their noses and put lotion on. Kids who watched *Video Soul* after school and copied what they saw in the mirror. Darienne, deflated from the big-chested video vixen that she was just a few minutes before, decided to audition herself back in.

"IIIIIIIIII geee-iiitttt sooo, weak in the knees. . . ." she belted, trying and failing to execute the infinite motion of knees and hips that was the Butterfly. On "weak" she dipped as low as her wasted five-foot-long legs would allow and then tried thrusting her allegedly experienced pelvis forward. She was more moth than butterfly—specifically one buzzed off too many granny panties.

Naturally, we begged her to do it again and again and again. And she obliged, each time singing a lot more off-key and gyrating a lot more like a rusty washing machine. Someone grabbed her knees (a rare moment of physical contact that would only be repeated under extreme duress) and tried to manipulate them into a spectacle worthy of *Solid Gold* while the rest of us stared greedily, storing the mental image like a squirrel does nuts—this being before digital cameras. And like a twice-deported illegal on an inner tube, Darienne kept coming back for more. Already a citizen, I felt sorry for her only in the most intangible of ways. We were sisters, right? Therefore this was all in good fun under the purview of . . . sibling rivalry, if you will. If you won't, then we were just bullies with lip gloss, ready to smack down on anything with less shine.

"Okay, one more time. Seriously, I think you've almost got it."

"IIIII geeee-iittttt, sooooooooo . . ."

That song would've been on repeat all night if it wasn't for Adaoha scratching up the record with a pointed "Darienne." The three of us froze in place like how you do in musical chairs, Darienne sitting back down in front of the computer. The only seat left; I guess she won. Adaoha, who we thought had been busy cramming, eyed the three of us with something worse than contempt, breaking whatever spell had been cast. Turning Darienne back into a bumpkin and us, her evil stepsisters. Mood. Killed. We sat down on the floor reluctantly, unwilling to admit our defeat or our crime. Nobody asked her.

The story would get mangled over time like a bad game of telephone. We teased her about what a misguided compassionate she once was. How she'd still be stuck living in Plimpton with the lesbians of Barnard wearing Old Navy cargo pants if we hadn't saved her from being too good. "Adaoha was such a dork before we rescued her," we'd say.

When we put on our white dresses, we became sisters. Made Adaoha cool. Made her part of the black girls' club we'd joined ourselves so many years before. The four of us (Darienne would dump us in a semester) sealed together like Mormon wives. Because eventually everyone joined the club, grabbed a mask, and walked around like their feet and the ground didn't mix. Playing at being grown is what we were doing. Maybe Adaoha knew the truth. Maybe she was the only one not playing. Maybe she got winded.

We lost her to the wind in March. We lost her to these intangibles about strength versus weakness and perfection versus reality. We lost her because we never took the time to think about any of that shit before the call came: our good friend—our sister— had slit her wrist, taken a bottle of pills, tried to drown herself, and finally taken a leap of faith off a building. We lost her.

In these types of situations, old people on TV always say something like "She looks good." She did not look good. She looked dead, with pink nail polish. I wanted to touch her hand but decided against it. I couldn't remember the last time I'd touched Adaoha. The last time I hugged her. Adrienne kept saying it would be okay. My throat was too sore to tell her to shut up. Kia let me lay my head on her lap, her pregnant belly taking up most of it.

Whatever happened next was all snow and static. Unwatchable.

There was a slide show at the repast, French for force-feeding your sorrow with baked chicken and nonalcoholic iced tea. Through the awesome power of PowerPoint, her life flashed before our eyes like we were the ones dying. Microsoft was never so macabre.

The last slide was stolen from her Facebook page. Adaoha took the time to change her profile picture before she left. Thoughtful. In it, she looked small. The camera is too far away, making her shoulders seem shy, her face sweet and childish. She is none of these things anymore. Was none of those things. I want never to see this picture again but am too superstitious to remove her from "friends." While contemplating this, Adrienne leans over to tell me that Paul, one of Adaoha's two ex-boyfriends and an asshole, told one of us that he alone knew "the real

Adaoha." I tell Adrienne I will deliver a roundhouse kick to his face. This is a funeral, not a who-knew-Adaoha-best dance-off. And if it were, we'd win. Obviously.

"I'm telling you, it's harder out here for us than it ever was for our mothers," I said out loud to no one in particular, the three of us stretched across my bed in our Sunday black. We stared up at the ceiling with our shoes off, watching the water stains as if they were clouds and wondering if we could have saved her somehow.

"Is it really, though?" asked Evelyn, another one of *us*, from the doorway. She was getting married in August.

"I think that shit makes sense," said Kia, from her side. Twenty-seven and pregnant with her third child (on the ride back to New York, she'd call to ask me to be the godmother), she looked doubly pathetic in funeral clothes. "When there's so many ways to go, it's easier to get lost, I guess. I don't know . . ."

What did we know? Like true Ivy League grads nothing worth a good goddamn. A bunch of cocktail-party chatter about the accomplishments of a woman we clearly never saw or would see again. She'd just bought a condo with granite countertops and West Elm furniture. She'd sold a tract of affordable houses out in Baltimore. She'd just gotten back from a trip to Brazil, where she shook her ass with the best of 'em. She'd joined Match .com and went on a date with a short African guy. She'd gone to a *bruja* once who told her marriage was in her future. She'd told me that Dex and I would work out someday. She'd broken my heart. What *did* we know?

◇◇◇◇◇◇

Weeks after the funeral, Adaoha's mother asked her friends in Washington to stop by her new/old condo and help clear things out. She was twenty-seven when she died, so this probably wouldn't take long. Her mom also wanted us to take some things with us, mementos or something.

On the twenty-minute metro ride there, Adrienne and I sat in silence. I shut my eyes once we pulled into the PG Plaza station. She asked me if I was okay about a zillion times. *Yes, yes, I'm fine.* I'd been sleeping with the lamp next to my bed turned on, a red scarf draped over it. The dark simply wouldn't do. I was as far from fine as any one person could get.

Her mom had pizza and chicken wings waiting. I grabbed a slice and went about the business of gathering up her Delta things in the black tote bag that was exactly like the one I had, but with Adaoha's name on it. I could joke with all her high school friends, but whenever Adrienne walked in with an old photo or a funny story from college, I'd leave the room or start inspecting my pepperoni. It was easy to act like we were throwing a surprise party and that Adaoha'd walk through the door shouting, "Loooosers," any minute. But I was stingy with my real grief. After we finished, I couldn't look inside the bag or in Adrienne's eyes.

◇◇◇◇◇◇

"Because life gets you fucked up, and you need some clarity from an uninvolved party." Gina was preaching therapy again. I was kind of sorry I brought it up.

When Adrienne called a few days later—we were all on this "check-in" thing now—I answered with a gruff, "Whaddaya-wan?"

"Hello," she said, ignoring my bitchy welcome. "I'm alive, in case you were wondering! Some best friend you are. You're supposed to be checking on my sanity." It was already summertime, and she was studying for the bar.

"Ummmm . . ."

"Which I'm COMPLETELY losing, by the way!"

"I have my own damn sanity to worry about. Thanks." I thought this might get her to hang up.

"What's wrong with you? What's wrong with your sanity?"

"Nothing's wrong with me." How could I tell her what I didn't know?

"Oh, so you're just being stanky."

Silence.

"Well—" She sighed. "I see you woke up on the wrong side of the bed . . . just saying hello."

"Dude, I'm working on a story that's due. I'm trying to keep my job, so I have a fucking career. And I hate everyone! Jesus. Can I live?" Maybe she'd leave me alone now.

"Like I said, just saying hello. You can go back to your dry v-wedgie now."

Everybody's got a thing. Kia talks to strangers. Adrienne's from Hah-lum! I'm a nomad. Adaoha? She had a dry v-wedgie.

If it sounds uncomfortable, that's because it's supposed to. We had no clue what a dry one actually felt like but imagined it involved vaginal friction equal to corduroy-on-corduroy action. If this sounds pornographic, it's not supposed to. The dry v-wedgie is more like an aphorism. *A v-wedgie stings for but a moment, a dry v-wedgie for a lifetime.* Basically, it's about spinsterhood. The first warning sign of that apocalypse. It was a joke, and Adaoha, our good friend and sister, had the misfortune of being its butt.

It started like this. We were two years out of college and at another one of Kia's baby showers. One little girl in attendance was wearing a pink corduroy jumpsuit that was too constrictive. In an effort to escape, she kept yanking it toward her chest as if it were a tearaway, the force of which created what can only be described as baby camel toe. No one saw but me. I tried to get her to stop violently exposing the outline of her little vah jay jay, but she was insistent, outlining the tiny V shape with each pull. "Okay, that's enough," I said gently, bending down to lift her little hands out of the pockets of her one-piece.

"She has a v-wedgie!" shouted some six-year-old in eyeshot.

"Excuse you?"

"A V-WED-GIE"—exasperated now, she was shouting like how you do with someone who doesn't speak the same language as you—"it's when—"

"Umm . . . I know what a v-wedgie is, little girl." I had no idea what a v-wedgie was, and neither should a first-grader. I shooed both of them—the v-wedgee and the v-wedger—into the next room for more fruit punch and innocence.

A few weeks later, we were having an alcohol-fueled debate on men—why we wanted 'em, where to find 'em, how to keep 'em. Adaoha, twenty-three, was a virgin then, or something close. It was my opinion that as soon as some dude got past her bra, all moral authority would go the way of the underwire. She ignored this and instead ticked off her list of requirements for happily-ever-after in old-school MASH style. Remember? Mansion, House, Apartment, Shack. Adaoha wanted a man with a degree, a six-figure salary, perfect teeth, a good family, a healthy 401K, and who would be ready to get married after a year of dating (and perhaps not doing it).

"What if you meet some gorgeous garbage collector or a street sweeper whose penis is like ten inches long?" I asked.

"Nope!"

"Boooooo. Just wait until some dude licks your titties. It's gonna be Reynolds for you, honey—a wrap, done, finito." At least that's how it was for me. All my onward-Christian-soldier brainwashing in Awanas came out in the wash once Gary Johnson convinced me to just let him "put the head in."

"I'm friggin' serious," Adaoha said. "I'm not going to settle for some ole bullshit." She beat back our barrage of explanations (the ones we'd been telling ourselves): there weren't that many college-educated black men on the market in the first place, and those who *were* on the auction block wanted white women or ghetto girls or men, not bourgie broads. A good black man wasn't just clandestine, he was near Jurassic. We were twenty-three and jaded.

But Adaoha wasn't—then. She'd skipped born-again trips to health services ("Please, God, if I'm okay this time then . . .") and reality checks before dawn ("Soooo, you're not staying over?"). I couldn't let her get away with being the me before I got grown and a prescription for Ortho. I wanted her down in the dumps with the rest of us. Back in the black girls' club.

"Well, then, you have fun with your dry v-wedgie!" I shot back.

There was a vacuum of silence and shocked looks right before the table burst into epiphany-strength laughter. DRY V-WEDGIES! This would be Adaoha's new epithet and our new rallying cry. Whenever heartbreak conned one of us into hating men, all anyone had to do was mention the word *dry* together with *v-wedgie*. Most closely translating to the phrase "Open sesame," "dry v-wedgie" unlocked visions of a nightmarish future where we spent each day racing through life with our heads down and our legs strong but all that chafing in between.

Maybe that's what Adaoha was thinking about the night she left us. We had our last conversation the day before.

JamAmPrincess (12:30:33 p.m.): Uh, what's with the piss face

nyCALlgrl4 (12:32:45 p.m.):   no more Dex

JamAmPrincess (12:33:45 p.m.): what y?

JamAmPrincess (12:34:08 p.m.): y r u makin it sound so final

JamAmPrincess (12:36:26 p.m.): ppl get back together

nyCALIgrl4 (12:36:32 p.m.): nope

nyCALIgrl4 (12:36:36 p.m.): we break up too much

JamAmPrincess (12:37:02 p.m.): ur still not telln me what happened

nyCALIgrl4 (12:37:06 p.m.): he doesnt want a relationship

nyCALIgrl4 (12:37:17 p.m.): nothing "happened" per se

JamAmPrincess (12:38:02 p.m.): so no more friends either?

nyCALIgrl4 (12:38:23 p.m.): i'm so not into s&m

JamAmPrincess (12:38:34 p.m.): lmao!

JamAmPrincess (12:38:59 p.m.): i'm just sayn mayb he's on a diff schedule

JamAmPrincess (12:44:42 p.m.): but u guys seemed so comfy together

nyCALIgrl4 (12:44:46 p.m.): we are

nyCALIgrl4 (12:47:28 p.m.): but he's so schizo about it

nyCALIgrl4 (12:47:36 p.m.): one second he wants to introduce me to his parents

nyCALIgrl4 (12:47:46 p.m.): and the next he's still hollering at this other chick

JamAmPrincess (1:02:49 p.m.): the one he was canoodling with in the club?

nyCALIgrl4 (1:07:05 p.m.): GIRL YES

She wasn't online the next day. Had already logged off. In real life I couldn't forgive her. Wouldn't. Or myself for letting her sign out without a warning. Something. I couldn't help thinking she had a secret. It made me jealous. Maybe what it really was: a surprise. Buried at the bottom of her bag. A lot of good that would do me: I was still too scared to look.

RUHBUHDUH

There comes a time in every twenty-seven-year-old's life when one realizes that the space between dormitory and factory has folded unflattering crow's feet into one's social life. Gone are the days when friends are an elevator ride away, dinner plans are made on the way to somebody's hall, and Thursday is Friday or Friday is Thursday (who cares, you'll figure it out in Philosophy C203). Dry-erase boards, once the standard-bearers of celebrity, are the vintage signboards of a bygone era: "Helena, me again. Just thought I'd remind you and that random guy you picked up about taking off your shoes. You spent the entire last Sunday cleaning footprints off your ceiling. Also please don't throw your condoms out of the window you're creating a small mountain. P.S. meet us in the dining hall at 7." Life is now a really misleading rerun of *Friends*, with no all-star cast and only one storyline— yours.

Soon enough, the little old lady living in a shoe is you—and the rent is effin' unbelievable, and nobody comes to visit because you're too far from the metro. Adulthood comes in little jigsaw pieces. Once the painstaking work of fitting them all together is done, the picture doesn't look nearly as cool as it did on the box. False advertising. But whom to sue? Jesus H. Christ?

Really, you should thank God for the gang of nerds who got together on their Segways and rode the information highway all the way to the bank, cashing in on our collective quarter-life crises, crisises, crisi. Making it impossible to stay mad forever, Facebook, MySpace, Gchat, LinkedIn, Skype, Twitter, and whatever people are doing now have each made this American life bearable for those of us on the too-in-touch-to-ever-be-nostalgic side of thirty. Actually, we all might be the unwitting participants of a controlled field study of the latest drug to battle Alzheimer's— *nevurfugetatal.*

What's the point of pontificating on the theoretical catechism, "Whatever happened to Randi Davidson?"—high school track star, wearer of purple lipstick to Prom, and face on a milk carton since senior night 1998—when suddenly her every move ("Randi Johnson is ready for date night with hubby!!!!!!") is shoved into your news feed quicker than you can say, "I bet you a million bucks she's gay now."

Where's the fun in playing fact or fiction when everybody knows the boring, nonpervy truth? And the ho-hum headlines break so fast you don't know which to pay attention to: "Aaron Ouyang just scored 8 out of 10 on his Sliders fanatics TV quiz," "Nicole Watson is thanking everybody for all the bday love," "Harry Chin is :(," "Adaoha Hamilton is hiding under her desk again," and "David Soriano is . . ." That last one is so fucking annoying—it's like, did you forget to type in that tedious tidbit that seemed so important three seconds ago or is correct conjugation that important to you? Fascist.

None of this is to say that I myself don't participate in the constant reel of unreasonable updates, adding my small change to the stock ticker along with all the other grown-ups bored out of their gourds. But at least I have the decency to set most of my crap to private, unleashing my ego fertilizer to "only friends."

The one time I showed up to my grandmother's $1 soul food restaurant in a "cropped sweater," she went nuts. "Lena, you're too young to have your stomach all out like that." At seventeen, I was wise enough not to laugh in her face, but stupid enough to say something like, "This is how people dress. It's the nineties, not olden times."

Nowadays, I would never wear anything baring my midriff and wish most people (especially plump ones) had Effie's conservative Compton values. Why not save something for later? And leave something for the imagination? Or better yet, make use of a highly advanced cow-cloaking device designed to keep 'em thirsty?

We don't have the time or the technology—that's why. So instead, the Jenga tower that is postjuvenile delinquency continues online, so that our offscreen affairs don't seem so lacking. An old friend once told me she wanted this other chick's "Facebook life," an oxymoron if there ever was one.

"She's got all these cool-sounding events on her page. Like every friggin' night there's something. I wanna go too. Would it be weird if I sent her a FB message like, 'Take me with you!' "

"First off, yes, Crazy Pants McGee," I said. "Second, get the heck outta here! It's not like she's actually going to any of these places. And, I'm sorry, does 'Grown and Sexy Saturdays at Saturna Italian Bar and Grille' really sound that awesome? No, ma'am." I was trying to be supportive.

"Whatever. Why aren't you on Twitter?"

"Because I'm not a fucking maniac." Again with the support.
"Since when?"

Later this same girl sent me and a whole bunch of other people she was either trying to impress or help get through the workday an e-mail with the subject line: "I'm famous." What followed was not an enthusiastic paragraph about her doctoral dissertation being accepted, but a link to a snarky Web site that posts particularly literary "tweets." Hers was first on the list: "The Ikea shuttle switches lanes like woah and drives over the double yellow line. Not so Captain Safety." I was proud in a Special Olympics type of way.

There is something to be said for the self-gratification felt in the presence of a group (or mass e-mail). The competing senses of purpose, accomplishment, and remorse.

Case in point: RBBDA. Street name: RuhBuhDuh. To its pushers: Rasheed's Black Bourgie Dating Advice. Yes, *that* Rasheed. "Raj," Britanya's ex. After I got rid of her in life, I picked him up in cyberspace. Not in a sexy way, but in a "Hey, the more guys I friend the higher probability I'll inadvertently meet a non-friend guy" kind of way. I considered falling in love with him one night after a friendly dinner at Clyde's, but then I figured it'd be easier to introduce him to my other friend Hillary, who wears pearls in the middle of the week by point of reference. Two jumbo lump crab cakes and six months later, they're in love. Even still, he remains dedicated to the cause of documenting the "exciting developments in the world of black bourgie dating" with his "just for fun" Facebook group, RBBDA.

Gina, at her dick's end, had an interesting theory on the educated-while-black dating scene: "I am just so tired of this shit. Like argh! Why don't they just keep a handful of men in a barrel, so that when one situation ends you just grab in there for another." Rasheed had his own suggestions. A fan of public displays of irritation, he got fed up and decided to tell the world according to Mark Zuckerberg about it.

A rhetorical note entitled, "Is bourgie black dating really that tough?" started everything. In it Rasheed answered his own question yes, and then told everyone he could tag why:

1. *The numbers are against us*—with only a fraction of the black population certifiable bourgie, it's hard to date healthy.

2. *The rest of the Blacks are against us*—Booker T. Washington and W.E.B. DuBois are more than the names across a booty-shaking high school band's parade banner.

3. *We're too career-oriented*—nobody works hard *and* plays hard. That's a dangerous myth made up by white people who like golf with their tequila.

4. *We take ourselves out of the game*—Grown and Sexy Saturdays at Saturna Italian Bar and Grille? Fail.

5. *The clusterfuck*—the only difference between bourgie dating and Appalachian inbreeding is the sea level.

6. *Robin Thicke*

At first it was just for shits and giggles. A silly list you might forward to your friends on a Friday before a working lunch at Fuddruckers. But eventually the comments section underneath unfurled like a red carpet. The road to social network stardom now clear, another note followed—"Bourgie Macking Week"— which included a maxim I adopted as my own, "Leave the hating ass friend at home." Sorry, Gi. Although I made sure to send her each of Rasheed's lists, because of course, another followed. The third and final note bore its header more like a headstone: "Bourgie Macking Week Failing!?! Dating Dead!?!" That's when shit got heavy, or at least a little chubby. Chances were getting slim that any of us girls would find *the one* for ourselves, since according to one comment, "I'm saying, meeting people clearly does not translate into dating. Because, in my experience, it is not hard to meet people in this city. But, I'm not convinced that dating exists in this city." This city being the nation's capital, and we, the people, being totally screwed.

Then, like rats on a sinking ship, we decided there was power in numbers and formed RBBDA, a Facebook "group for uppity black people to discuss dating, relationships, sex, and whatever else is on the mind." Of the 302 members, about 24 were doable in a classic sense. Most were from bourgie-approved locales like Washington, Atlanta, and Chicago. Rasheed dubbed himself "The Originator" and demanded that we go forth and mull over heady topics like: "The Champagne Brunch," "Your Standards Are Too High," "I Caught Him Peeing in the Shower," "Fuck Yeah, Dow Jones," and "Addicted to RBBDA."

I authored a few new topics myself, most notably one entitled "The Kinsey Scale," which I wrote after watching Liam Neeson, as real-life nerd-turned-sexpert Alfred Charles Kinsey, have movie intercourse with his straw-haired wife and manly researcher. Since he literally wrote the books on sex, I assumed we could have a robust debate about "the down low" and whether men having sex with men were gay. Thoughts? None.

They (I use the third person plural here in order to protect the innocent from any lame-doing) even planned a "conference" in D.C. that I reluctantly chose Netflix over only after a robust debate on which would be more productive. "Dude, you met these people on the Facebooks? What are you now, a forty-year-old white lady?" Gina did not approve. But then again, she was no less single than I was. RBBDA was planning a second conference, and I decided to take Raj's advice and "leave the hating ass friend at home."

RBBDA 2.0 was taking place in New York that summer. I gave a Chinese woman wearing a fanny pack thirty bucks for a ticket to Thirty-fourth Street on a charter bus that looked like it'd had a hard life. "You going New Yawk?" she asked, already herding me into the line of graduate students and staff assistants to Sen. Somebody. My bag was sentenced to the hull before I could answer, "Yes! I going New Yawk to find me a man." I grabbed a seat near a window, sat back, and watched *Mission Impossible II*.

Dexter and I were broken up, and this time I was serious about it. He said he had "weird in-between feelings" for me, so I was determined to get someone else between the sheets. Well, not really. The only one-night stand I ever had ended eleven months after with tears and a "what relationship?" So maybe I've never had one. Really, I just wanted to do enough heavy petting to warrant mentioning on Monday when Dex called to ask how my weekend with those "probably psycho-killer online sex chat friends" went. Because in-between feelings were still feelings, after all.

So. RBBDA. There were three distinct factions on "the boards": *newbies, regulars,* and *lurkers.* I was a semiregular with lurker tendencies. It seemed as if every thirty minutes spent working damaged my brain in such a way that I couldn't remember whether or not I'd checked the groups discussion board, wall, or news section that day. Trusting my gut, I'd get as far as "www.fa . . ." before my computer did the rest. Once inside, I spent the next hour reading posts, showing the pervier ones to my white work wife Emily, and then deciding not to make any potentially-harmful-when-my-husband-is-trying-to-win-Iowa comments of my own. That was the *lurker* in me—getting off on the sex diaries of others but remaining stingy with mine. To a certain extent. Once I did share a few lines about the time an old friend gave a valiant if brusque effort in a Los Angeles hotel room. But that was it. And the other time with a seven-foot college basketball star who could lift his leg behind his head and squeal like a gymnast half his size. Okay, fine, I was a perv too.

As such, I felt like I "knew" these "people," who up until now had been only thumbnails to me. But I wasn't a regular either. Despite evidence to the contrary, I did have a full-time job and a part-time life.

Of the regular chicks, there were five in New York: Justine, Tonya, Courtney, Reiko, and Dee. These were girls I'd never seen after five or in the flesh. On the guys' side there were Douglas, Van, Raj, Chris, and Stu—all super cute in miniature, like dollhouse furniture. Looking back, the black-and-white glamour shots should have tipped me off. Who takes a picture of just their eye?

After making it off the Chinatown bus with only the slightest case of SARS, I met up with the group at a dive bar in the West Village. The only people I'd met in the nonvirtual world were Hillary and Raj, who according to their text messages were somewhere in the back. A bunch of black people were holding court at the table nearest the front entrance. I tried to avoid eye contact, because being the new girl is a lost art, like climbing monkey bars and raising my hand. Checking my phone for the third time in as many seconds seemed like the better option. *I'm really in high demand and not a loser,* this pantomime was meant to say. *I have friends. They're just not here—yet. Because they, of course, are tardy and rude. I, on the other hand, am responsible and confident.* My phone rang in the middle of me fake-listening to a

ghost voice mail. As "Does that make me craaa-zaaay . . ." torpe-
doed down my ear, I pretended not to notice.

"Something's wrong with this damn phone," I told my face to
say. It was Rasheed. He'd spotted someone who looked like me
looking like an asshole and wanted to make sure. They were two
tables away. I couldn't see them past all the mixing, mingling,
and morbid obesity. Yeah, a lot of these girls were . . . healthier
than their thumbnail versions suggested. There was someone
that resembled Justine, who according to her profile pic was
often surprised mid–high kick. This real girl had missed a few
dance classes and added as many pounds. The before shots went
on from there like a Dexatrim commercial that'd been horribly
botched. *Geez, Larry, some idiot cut out the girls from Barbizon!* I
thought I saw someone who looked like Doug, but about a foot
shorter. Van's teeth were way bigger than useful; no wonder he
never smiled in his pics. Raj and Hillary, always a puke-inducing
example of bliss, were sucking a supersize something from the
same straw. I wished my brain was frozen too. Maybe I could
still catch the 11:00 p.m. back to the bat cave.

"Helena. Helena! Over here." Yes, these were the right people.
My people.

"This is horrendous." I needed to get that out before my butt
hit the seat Rasheed held out for me. I needed to make my dis-
satisfaction with real life known.

"Shut your face, dick towel," he said. "I've got someone for
you to meet."

I searched Hillary's face for approval. Finding none, I rolled
my eyes and tapped the waitress. "One of those slurpees for
lushes, please." I'd wasted three-inch heels.

This "someone" was a five-foot-four baldhead from New
Jersey, but who claimed Brooklyn instead. He had on the jeans

of a much taller/wider man and had mistakenly decided against a belt. Employing his left hand to that end, his right was busy with a highball of Courvoisier. Since neither was free to shake my hand hello, I got a head nod, delivered with all the bravado of a man twice his size. Oversize suit jackets will do that. I gave Rasheed the side eye before he left the two of us alone. Waiting three very polite beats, I excused myself to the ladies' room. Baldhead's eyes dug into the back of my neck as I tried and failed to disappear into the crowd. Was he willing me back, or working out the tools necessary for murder? I took my chance but didn't make it far.

"So you weren't going to say 'hi,' were you?" I'd recognize that sarcasm and sweater vest anywhere. One was patterned and the other practiced.

Derek was Rasheed's gay husband without the sex or social aptitude. Theirs was a love fashioned around boat shoes (without the socks) and seersucker. Derek and I shared an equally preppy night of the missionary position the year before. It was the first time I'd played shirts and skins in the bedroom. He kept his on. The. Entire. Time. Lifting the front hem over his head only when my eyes were closed (which they clearly weren't) in order to get some flesh on flesh as opposed to boobs on Hanes. The whole thing felt very gyno.

"Heeey, you," I said in the voice usually reserved for work functions. "What has your life been about?"

While Derek thumbed through his CliffsNotes—working in London, partner track, yachts—I drifted off to wherever bored hearts go. *Argyle probably felt funny against bare breasts, and this top wasn't so slutty I couldn't pull it off on the train tomorrow morning. His man boobs weren't so much bigger than mine that it'd be weird. If we left now . . .*

"See, Helena and I used to be lovers." I caught him mid-e.g., offering me up as an example on his sex CV to some chick with short hair and a pretty face who'd sidled up to our conversation while I was pipe-dreaming. Grateful that the mood had been murdered, I backed away real slow, pivoting just in time to catch Baldilocks giving me the squinty face from the bar. Again, I didn't know whether to be horny or horrified, so I chose both, but kept moving just in case.

Hillary, always anxious to set people up (for failure, I think), wanted to know what I thought.

"Of Weirdo McFeirdo over there?"

"He's been eyeing you all night." She was squealing.

"And this is a good thing? Please tell Rasheed that he's an epic failure and should log off of life immediately. What the hell was he thinking?"

"He said that you wanted a dude who, and I'm quoting you here, 'would punch me in the throat and say let's fuck.' So there you go," she said, making her arm into a teapot spout, boiling in the direction of Bald, James Bald.

"I can't begin to define sarcasm in a bar. Plus, if this cat wanted to grab my throat he'd have to leap like, I don't know, three feet. Raj could've at least picked someone who can give me a good thrashing on his own hemisphere."

To take my mind off things, we slurped down more frozen primary colors and talked about the debauchery waiting to happen. Dee was sharing a hotel room with Stu, who was presently getting a lap dance from someone who was not Dee. Apparently, Justine was a "squirter," which didn't surprise me, since I'd just witnessed her demonstrating what a "scorpion" looks like in cheerleading, gymnastics, and now dive bars. In brief, it is when one reaches behind one's back, grabs a foot, and pulls it up to one's head. Right. Squirting seemed like just another mundane display of physicality she'd share with the class. At least that's what she told Doug, who, despite his diminutive size, would hook up with three different girls that weekend. Derek? Zero. A fact that supremely vexed him and Courtney, who secretly hated me because she had a none-too-secret thing for Derek. We'd met more than once, and she always introduced herself anew like an amnesiac, thus proving the hatred theory, because I hate when people do that because you know they're just doing it to infuriate you, unless they, in truth, suffer from amnesia. Then it's just sad.

Truly pathetic was the fact that I treated these people like glitches in the system despite being right there with them, fucking up the connection with my supposed awesomeness. And still, I was the one walking to the train alone an hour later, deftly ignoring the "hey shawtays" of men eight feet tall sporting wife beaters that could hardly contain their protruding pecs. I wanted everything, but really only one thing. Sparks! "You just wanna be all up Dex's booty," was Adrienne's analysis. I had my doubts about the prevalence of sparks in there, but saw her point. It took another year for me to get my head out of his ass and back to where it all started.

Took me a year to remember the truth behind Rasheed's very first note. The list of the reasons why it was hard to be bourgie and black. No. 5: The clusterfuck. "And even more common is the fact that we've often developed platonic relationships with opposite sex folks, who if we were just meeting them, we might pursue amorous intentions with, but because we've been friends for so long, that's off the table. Or we already dated their monkey ass, and it didn't work out." RBBDA became required source material. If I was going to get a life, or at least get *some* (since everyone else was, even Justine, the high-kicking squirter), I'd need some guidelines.

I reread the old post, "I've Got a Crush on You," which attempted to spell out the ABCs of turning a homey to a husband. Scrolling through two pages of responses, I was surprised to find my own name among the "experts." What I had to say was profoundly pointless: "There's a fine line between putting yourself out there and playing yourself." No shit, Sherlock. Last year's me had nothing but craptastic advice for this year's version, because it never works that way around, except for in *Encino Man*.

I needed advice, because there was this new guy, Jake—an old friend I met through older friends, who after several thousand lines of chat, finally delivered a jewel, "I have two moods: happy and pissed off." Lust. Ignited. Actually, it was Frances, my mother, who lit the match, describing him twice as having a "nice build," which obviously grossed me out at first and then at second made me think. Soon I was spending an extra ten minutes in bed every morning, fantasizing about this nice build of his and how it would look erect. I e-mailed a new-boy alert to Adrienne and Gina with the disclaimer that nothing could ever happen because we were in the friends zone—the danger zone.

"So did you tell Jake you want to ride his pony yet?" Adrienne's nicknames for anatomy rival an eight-year-old's.

"I do not. Shut your mouth, monkey breath!"

"Umm-hmmm."

I hung up on her and immediately got back to my life according to Gchat.

ME: I break out in hives whenever I'm really stressed. Guess what's all over my back?

[Appropriate conversation in mixed company]

JAKE: Sexy, sexy.

ME: LMAO. Not boils. This isn't medieval times.
Although I'd love to go there.

[Not that I'm fishing for an invitation]

JAKE: How can you alleviate this stress? Need anything?

[*Is* this an invitation?]

ME: Besides a vibrator?

[Hope so]

JAKE: I'll pick one up for you.

[Dear God.]

ME: Get outta town.

[Or in my pants]

JAKE: Dude, if you need one I got you.
I'm secure enough to stop at the store.
And buy a giant black cock for you.
I mean, I'd prefer to bring a pizza, but whatever.

Waiting for pepperoni and black olives never hurt so good. I wore a V-neck with no bra and jeans with no shoes. This was casual. What's a slice of pizza and an episode of *Seinfeld* among friends? Then again, isn't this how things always go down in the pornos? Pizza guy, girl with no panties, a six-pack, the TV's on but no one watching, and then bowchickabowbow!

We typed on our laptops for a few hours, me hoping he was messaging someone about the fraught sexual tension between the cushions of my very grown-up couch. And he, redacting top-secret legal mumbo-jumbo, totally unaware of my uptight nipples.

That's when I decided all Ruhbuhduh really was, was just a lot of gibberishishy gobbledygooked hogwash. A bunch of grown-ups trying to grow their own luck. Ruhbuhduh Shmuhbuhduh, might as well be Pig Latin for "Go fuck yourselves, 'cause nobody else is going to."

TRANNYGATE

Only once in my life have I ever wished for a time machine—or, lacking the technology, a driver's license.

It was Christmas in Los Angeles, which despite not looking much different than any other time is, indeed, special. I'd spent nearly a decade out on my own—even going so far as to tilt my "west sii-ide" the 90 degrees it took to claim the east—but California was still called "home." There'd always be one week at the end of December when the weather was in the high eighties and time was frozen in the late nineties. Not only was I back, but *we* were. Gina knew all the old stories I only wanted to hear in L.A., my grown-up lullabies. Like that time Richard Shin threw a "bomb" made of water and single-ply from the second-floor boy's bathroom onto Janet Lalebekeyan's back and then she bitch-slapped him with the same wet toilet paper in front of *everybody.* Everybody was small enough to fit in a carry-on that week. Actually, everybody was just me and Gi.

I think *we* all started after I went away to college. She started calling to talk about the gorgeous eggheads I'd be meeting. Fools that we were. Eventually we became more than each other's sounding boards—we were each other's wailing walls. Whenever I got back into town, there was only one question: "Dude, what are we doing *esta noche?*"

On this particular break "we" now included a new dude named Bilal. She wanted me to meet him, and instead of being envious, I was excited. Too bad he left me wishing for a pimped-out DeLorean capable of turning back time to before the night started.

The three of us were having drinks at the bar/lounge in the Sofitel off Wilshire Boulevard near the Beverly Center. A glass of Riesling was $16, but we weren't college or even graduate students anymore, so fuck it. Gina and Bilal had fallen in love a few months before, after a day spent in bed watching *Clue*—her favorite movie of all time, next to *our* favorite, which is *Teen Witch*. Unable to top his unflinching knowledge of *Clue*'s complete working script, Gina gave Bilal a pass on being half African.

A brief note on xenophobia and dating: when you're from Los Angeles, where one is either black or Mexican, not Martian, your opinion of people opposite the globe is formed almost exclusively by the movie *Not Without My Daughter*. Forged in the fires of Lifetime, *NWMD* is a film about race, religion, family, abuse, divorce, escape, and Sally Field's convincing hijab. Basically, she marries a doctor who happens to be Iranian (as played by Alfred Molina) and everything's all lovey-dovey until he takes her and their kid to Tehran and then goes bat shit crazy after praying or something. In the end, Field plus her daughter escape on a magic carpet, kind of. Anyway, the movie also doubles as code word for racism in romance if, finding ourselves in mixed company, we need to express fears over a potential partnering of one with an *other*.

"Ooh, look at Punjabi MC being all sexy at the bar. Hol-laaaaaah. . . ." one of us might say in reference to an attractive gentleman of South Asian descent.

Cutting her off after a quick up-and-down, the other might reply, "Dude. Not. Without. My. Daughter." And the issue would get tabled—indefinitely. Gina's looking past Bilal's African-ness was huge, therefore prompting me to utter the phrase, "I like him for you."

Third-wheeling it suddenly didn't seem so bad. She was super hyped about a guy, and I wanted to bask in some of the after-glow. Unfortunately, my time in the spotlight was all too brief.

Okay, there was a tranny at the bar who kept eyeing Bilal. Gina pointed her out. When he (Bilal, not the she-man) walked over to chat it up with her (the tranny), we were horrified. The scoop was that the tranny (name unnecessary) was in fact a real live thirty-five-ish woman with whom Bilal had done some things. How we came to find out this information I was never sober enough to know, but once it was revealed, there was no stopping the onslaught. Also I don't think she looked so abso-lutely mannish—there were some very women-of-the-WWF thighs and a pair of arms that would decimate Angela Bassett's in *What's Love Got to Do with It*—but nothing that would place her last in the LGBT acronym marathon. But Gina said, so I went with it.

"They didn't do it or anything," Gi reported back after inter-rogating Bilal over by the men's room. "But they got close. Made out, but didn't do it. I was like, 'Oh word,' and he was like, 'It was a bad look. I was drunk.' He admitted the folly of his ways—immediately." *Fine, can we go back to talking about* my *life now?*

We'd been pounding Rieslings for about three hours. The last lick of the scoop was that Bilal and the tranny were only one naked sexy time removed, meaning that this was the chick delivering the goods before Gina got the job. I won't say she was jealous, but she was definitely something close. My job as the best friend was to deflect. "Dude, look at her." Knock back. "Puhlease, she's hideola!" Swig. "What the hell are they over there gumming it up about? Prostate cancer?" Chug-a-lug. When it finally came time to pack up our stink eyes and head home, I won't say we were drunk as fuck, but we were definitely close.

There's something that happens at the end of any night when a nondriver has been driven to some far-off locale—Beverly Hills, say—by a driver who has found herself exhausted by drink. Call it the whispering hour. It's when the driver slurs to whomever's closest, *Who's taking [social retard who can't drive] home?*

Fortunately, since 1996, Gina and I have never had to suffer through the faked loss of hearing necessary for the nondriver to survive the whispering hour. The term *gas money* was Greek to me, but my lack of language skills never seemed to bother her. Whenever the lights came up, dunking whatever club in vampiric mace, I'd never have to pretend-hail a cab or ask who was heading my way—Gi was *always* heading my way.

With Tranny gone and the lights on, Gina, Bilal, and I waited for the valet to bring The Explorer around front (Gina's Ford Explorer has been around for more than a decade, earning through sheer guts the respect of a direct article). Standing far enough away that I didn't vomit from their cuddling but still close enough to make it obvious I needed a ride, I may have heard the soft grumbling of a quiet riot against taking me all the way across town to my grandma's, but promptly dismissed it. *Where to next, guys?* When I climbed into the backseat, though, the nonsexual tension was thicker than the Tranzilla's thighs, which is to say impossible to ignore.

Me playing dead wasn't working. Through the white noise of passive-aggressive mumbling from the passenger's side (a spot already molded to my cheek specifications, but whatevs), it was clear that Bilal was pissy about something. *Were we back on the tranny thing? Come on guys, give it a rest.* I thought it best to decrease my surface area and disappear into the leather. While I spent the next couple of lights dissecting deserted sidewalks, attending the beat-up skin around my thumbnails, and knuckle-ironing my club jeans, the game of chicken happening in front reached critical mass.

"Drop me off, then." His fingers already gripping the trigger.

"Whatever." Her nerves already shot.

"I'm serious."

Now, I've been accused by lesser beings of being a touch narcissistic, but this *was* actually about me. Boiled down to the basics, Bilal didn't want Gina driving me home, presumably because she was drunk, but probably because he wanted her naked at his house posthaste. He actually suggested I take a cab. She suggested he shut the hell up.

Then he was all, Drop me off. And she was all, Sure. And he was all, No, really. And she was all, Fine, Bilal. The whole scene was ripped from the pages of our ninth-grade yearbook—the one where Gina wrote, "KIT this summer and don't let these dudes get you down. Keep ya head up ☺" They were still one-upping each other when Bilal took whatever the opposite of a chill pill was and, hopped up on misguided courage, flung open the car door. While. The Explorer. Was still. In motion.

"What the fuck are you doing?!"

"Let me out," he yelled, pretty pointless, since technically some of him was already out.

Gina busted a U-ie across four lanes of traffic and screeched up to the nearest stretch of curb. Then Bilal, open car door still in hand, leaped out without saying a word. The silence woke me up.

"Dude, what the—"

"Fuck it," she said, staring straight ahead like a woman possessed, or one pissed the hell off.

To describe this new turn of events as awkward would not be understatement. It would be criminally negligent. First off, now I'm being chauffeured around like an overscheduled six-year-old on her way to yet another play date, while Gina—now cast as the overextended BlackBerry mom—barrels down Wilshire Boulevard, daydreaming about how different her life might be without the brat in the back. The weightlessness would take some getting used to, but at least she'd be free. More than a cock blocker, I was a relationship millstone. And it only took me a few hours.

We headed in the opposite direction of wherever it was Bilal dared himself out of the car. He was behind us somewhere, getting swallowed up by the L.A. night or propositioned by its employees. Four morphed into five morphed into six on the radio minute hand before either of us said anything.

"Dude, what the—" I felt that that needed some repeating.

"Dude, I can't." What she couldn't didn't need repeating.

"We can't just leave him back there." Note here the casual usage of the royal "we," most often bandied about by those packing a nondriver ID. "How's he getting home?" Equally disingenuous, the nondriver always worries about how others are getting home even though she can do absolutely nothing useful in the situation seeing as how she, in title and definition, is a useless member of society. Even more applicable, the manless best friend always fucks shit up and then wonders aloud how to fix it.

"He said drop him off, so I dropped his ass off."

"Jesus."

Staring her down, I compelled her into turning around before we'd driven so far away it'd be a waste to go back—he'd either be

murdered or too mad. We pulled up near the corner and parked
where Bilal went all Evel Knievel on us. He was at the bus stop
now, lounging on a bench like he belonged there, wanted to be
there.

"Go get him," said Gina to the Helena reflection.

"Fuck!" replied Helena back to the car mirror.

I should also mention that at this moment in time I'd known
Bilal for maybe eight hours, give or take however many times
we'd exchanged cell phone "hi's" to the other in the background.
Now it was my job to convince a known daredevil that although
getting back in the car would be less exciting than hanging out
on Beverly and Wilshire, it'd probably be more dangerous. Plus,
I didn't think the buses even ran that late, and obviously he
didn't have money for a cab, or else he'd have given it to me.
Before Bilal would get off the bench, he had to say that Gina
made bad decisions, and by this point I was inclined to agree.
But since I *was* the bad decision, I kept my mouth shut and gave
him an "Umm-hmm" instead. I did, however, mention something about him being totally right, Gina being totally drunk,
and it being totally 2:00 a.m. Years from now, they'd be telling
2.5 kids this story. *Good thing Helena was there!* On the walk of
blame back to The Explorer, I gave Bilal the new rules of engage-
ment: no judging, no whispering, and definitely no leaping from
moving vehicles—at least until I was out of the car. Then off to
grandmother's house we went.

Everything was pretty normal for a while, if normal's definition is ass-numbing silence. Up front, I'm sure the two of them
were busy practicing whatever speech they planned to deliver to
the other in the morning. In my head, I was volunteering to take
a damn cab or at least sleep on somebody's bumpy couch. *You
two kids work it out in the bedroom, I'll be fine right here.* But I
knew Gina wouldn't let me. Because by now it was the principle

of the thing. She was going to drive me home no matter the cost—relationship, gas money. I wanted to tell her something, anything, to make all this weirdness disappear, but I left it alone.

Eventually they did get into a debate of stage whispers about what bad decisions Gina made—namely, having me as a friend. Actually, I'm just assuming that last part, since I was playing possum in the back so well I forgot I existed, which was probably for the best.

The universe, or more tangibly the Los Angeles Police Department, has a way of reminding us of such things. The time machine would've come in handy right about now.

The scene was Manchester Avenue, a stretch of depressed gravel that kisses the Pacific Ocean to the west and tongues down Inglewood on the east. It's familiar and old. Like most Los Angeles streets south of anything good, it belongs to the '60s on a clear day and the late '80s on a smoggy one. Earlier Bilal had mentioned something about there being drunk-driving dragnets on Manchester right across from the cemetery and next to the Forum—where huge crowds of screaming fanatics used to worship the Lakers and now do the same for the Lord. But since the general consensus inside The Explorer was that Bilal was a damn maniac who opened the doors of moving vehicles, we shut him down before he even got started.

We should have listened.

"What's with the traffic? It's like three in the freaking morning," I asked the Stupid Questions fairy outside my window.

"Is that a cop?"

"Perfect."

We couldn't see the whole thing until Gina pulled up to her place in the line to get fucked. The stoplight, blinking red like a silent alarm, flashed everything into obviousness—cops in cop cars, clipboards, mobile booking units that made me think of temporary classrooms, tow trucks, poor unfortunate souls trying to pat their heads while rubbing their tummies, and the absence of hope. One uniformed gentleman walked up to Gina's window, did the international hand sign for "Roll your window down, your best friend just ruined your record," and asked her if she'd had anything to drink. She said, "No." I imagined we'd get the same cell, but one never knows.

"You sure, ma'am?" he asked, giving her an eye exam with the flashlight buried in his palm.

"Well, just a glass of wine or two." This was so ballsy it made my mouth water. I swallowed with a guilty gulp, remaining silent without having to be told.

"Ma'am, can you pull your car around the corner here." Politeness while being policed is offensive. And since peeling off in a cloud of smoke down Manchester and to my grandma's for a new pair of panties and then maybe on to Mexico was out of the question, so was defending ourselves. I couldn't protect Gina, and it seemed as if Bilal just didn't want to. He planted an elbow against the passenger door, resting his chin on his balled fist and rolling his eyes. Teaching her some kind of lesson, I suppose.

Another uniformed gentleman took Gina away to do all the choreographed calisthenics you see on *Cops*. Thank God she'd decided against heels. While she aped drunken *Darrin's Dance Grooves* outside, I was going ape-shit inside. They were about to take her down to Chinatown! And it was all my fault—sort of. I promised baby Jesus I'd buy the ten-lesson package from Drive Right as soon as I got back to Washington—*just please don't force her to fashion a shank out of her Shu Uemura eye pencil.* As I begged our Lord and Savior to spare Gina from a life of checking "yes" to the crime conviction question on any application, Bilal reached into his back pocket and pulled out his PalmPilot. *Bilal has JC on speed dial?* Nope, but he does have a saved game of Solitaire.

"What the hell are you doing?!" I said, wedging my head into the space between him and his home screen. Visual confirmation complete. This dude was in fact playing a game designed specifically for octogenarians and eighth-graders while the woman he told me he loved (again, we'd known each other for one-third of a day) was pivoting with her left foot on the imaginary line, dividing the us of right now from whatever we were before an acronym made everything all blurry. DUI. Don't underestimate incompetence. What was bizarre about this entire situation, aside from the fact that an innocent Riesling-induced rage had spun way out of control, was how damn nonchalant Bilal was acting about the whole thing. As if Gina and I both had brought this on ourselves. As if the two of us together were the problem. Maybe one without the other would have a chance.

Every good friend just wants to be needed by the other, until she's not because a penis has come between them. Then when the thing goes limp, she's needed again, and whatever condescension she feels is fleeting, wiped clean by the righting of the order of things. This was how it was supposed to be, right? Just me and Gina. I hated him for making me feel so damn useless.

"Well, there's nothing we can do right now," Bilal said without looking up from the stacks of cards smaller than Chiclets in his hand. He was serious. This was happening. I was being voted *Most Likely to Have to Get Her Shit Together When Boyfriend Loses His* without having to hand out cupcakes or oversize buttons.

"Are you insane? We need to figure out what we're going to do if they arrest her ass," I said, squinting my eyes in the rearview, trying to make out if the objects therein appeared bigger than they actually were. I mean, were we really in the shit? Was Gina going to do time, or at the very least suffer major bureaucratic inconvenience, because I was too busy for a driving lesson ten years before?

"Oh, they're *going* to arrest her," Bilal announced, without pity. Great, a card game enthusiast and a pessimist.

As far as rescue teams go, Bilal and I sucked. Lacking the positive energy necessary to secret her out of those handcuffs and back in the driver's seat, we spent the next half hour debating whether or not Gina (a) brought this on herself, (b) would get out of this unscathed, or (c) would be not only scathed but scared shitless. He kept the time by tapping black and red cards across the screen with his stylus. I drummed the backbeat against my window, watching to make sure she wasn't getting brutalized—or worse, videotaped.

A rap on the windshield threw us off. Yet another Mr. Officer, Sir—this one kind of sexy in that lame Bachelorette Party stripping-to-get-through-med-school sort of way, did I mention it'd been a long time?—came over to smash my pipe dreams: Gina was in a mobile home being booked under the suspicion of drunk driving. Her continued refusal to take a breathalyzer test (more balls!) would most definitely end in a one-way ticket down to Chinatown. Population: alarming. Praise Jesus, there was a conjunction in there somewhere. If one out of the two of us had a California driver's license, they could release her to our custody, and this whole thing would play out in the fluorescent light of day court. Otherwise, The Explorer was on its way to wherever irresponsible cars go for a time-out. Since Bilal was from Ohio, and I was from Idiot Island, our last card got played before the game even started. No, we couldn't talk to her. No, we didn't have much time.

Was there someone, a real adult maybe, into whose custody they could release her? Yes, yes! I called Frances, who showed up in PJs and Asics. Bilal called his roommates, Jewish guys doing the scriptwriting thing. Oh, wait, did we mention that only The Explorer's registered owners can save it from the tow truck?

Crap. I was trying to avoid calling Jane and Carl, Gina's parents, at all costs. There was a time in eleventh grade when Gi told her mom she was with me when in fact she was with a college guy until well after midnight curfew. By the time sixteen-year-old Gina finally got home, the always-appropriate Jane, who'd been waiting on their manicured lawn in a terry-cloth robe, said, "Ass." I didn't want to be the jackass at the beginning of that sentence. So using the 3:00 a.m. voice, my opening line for talking to Jane had been passed down over the centuries from fuckup to fuckup: "We're okay. . . ."

But were we? I knew I was, and Bilal, who all during the wait to be rescued by people obviously more qualified managed to stack all his cards up in a row, had to be too. It was the "we" part that had me all messed up. Without me, Gina would be on the opposite side of the universe right now, in a place called her boyfriend's arms, oblivious to the fact that she had a selfish bitch for a BFF and a possibly autistic asshole for a boyfriend. Solitaire for a straight hour? Really, guy?

Even if I had the DeLorean, the flux capacitor, and all the gigawatts to get us out of here, Doc only knows when I'd program it for—1996 and Melrose Driving School? To Pilgrim High School in 1994, when the sporty girls needed a fifth and Gi picked me? Two hours ago on the corner of Wilshire, or a day ago when Gina said she wanted me to meet Bilal: "All right, you gotta see this dude and tell me what the deal is." Helena from today would have tried to convince the Helena from yesterday to say something sincere or white girl–ish like, "If you like him then I like him. I'm sure he's perfect!" And when the old Helena rolled her neck around to give me the side eye and ask, "Why the hell . . . ?" the time-traveling Helena would cut her off with the YouTube of right now and say, "This is why, bitch!" Then the happy couple in the picture would fade back into existence, minus the annoying friend holding up bunny ears behind them. Then the present day would be even better than before. Or . . .

Maybe all of this was a good thing. Well, not the whole DUI situation—everyone can agree how much that was going to hurt come tomorrow morning—but perhaps by some convoluted cosmic kismet, my lack of a driver's license had inadvertently outed Bilal's lack of common sense. I mean, why didn't he just drive? Why didn't the three of us just head to his house, which was like ten minutes from the bar, and sleep off our troubles? But see, someone in possession of a nondriver's ID cannot ask these types of questions from the backseat. It isn't done. Also, what kind of sociopath plays solitaire when his girlfriend might be in solitary? It didn't take long for me to diagnose Bilal with Asperger syndrome. I was rescuing Gina from having "special" children. Screw my promises to Mr. J. H. Christ: not driving was saving more souls than the Forum on Sundays.

In the time it took for me to absolve myself, the cavalry had arrived. Frances came first, walked straight up to Gina at the mobile home moonlighting as the intake center, gave her a wink, and said, "It's all good." Then she gave Gina her shoulder, and the two of them stood still for a minute. Then came Bilal's white boys from Hollywood. And then Carl and Jane, who, just wanting their daughter back, decided to hold the furious for later. I was all set to roll down my window and yell, "It wasn't me!" but thought better of it. Whichever way the steering wheel turned, it *was* me. I'd helped rack up negative points on her driving record and added yet another name to the losing column of her love life because, obviously, I'd have to inform her of what a jerk Bilal had been this whole time. She should probably dump me, though—trade me to some East Coast team where nobody passed me the ball. Trying for one last Hail Mary, before everybody got to The Explorer, I gave Bilal the score.

"Don't say shit to her. All that other bullshit that happened before—forget about it, for now at least. She's had handcuffs put on her. She is now a person that has been handcuffed. Her whole life is a shambles." I was talking fast, hoping he was catching some of it, any of it.

"All right," he said, sounding annoyed.

I wish I could say he'd put down his phone.

Fourteen

G.H.E.I.

File this under G.H.E.I.:

Cardigans in Mister Rogers red, size *smedium*, hyper nipple awareness, the flexibility to lift one's five-foot-long legs over one's head, squealing, combat boots, jeans with stretch, eurocentricity, K-Swiss sneakers, fat laces, pashmina, limes in Corona, Corona, the phrase "I love modern dance," exclamation points, squealing, white linen, flip-flops, guy gauchos, cashiering at Barneys CO-OP, sexy face, DSLs, overactive hands, overarched eyebrows, BeDazzling, working on one's personal relationship with Jesus Christ, light eyes, briefs, boat shoes, the facedown jockey position, a plastic pink butt replica hidden underneath a West Elm bed, Amsterdam, acting classes, sarging, Express Men, eye-rolling, and squealing. One hundred words on why we never win, by Gina Albertson.

"Dude, I can't with you and these gay dudes," she said, frustrated by the exponential growth of the questionably queer database I call the G.H.E.I. file so we can speak about it in public without offending the actual gays. "Seriously."

"James is so not gay. He's just . . . eurocentric. In France he'd be totally normal, masculine even. Uber. Masculine!" We were a day past Inauguration 2009, and to commemorate, I'd decided that James and I should get married. His dad was from Africa and he grew up in Arkansas, and I was from the south side of California. We were a campaign ad waiting to happen, but for his apparently conspicuous attraction to men as evidenced, according to Gina, Inspector Gayness, by his smedium skintights.

"Those pants aren't even that bad. He's got some way sexier."

"Sexy or suspect, dude? But it's whatever, 'cause I'm uberly familiar with your protocol. Uberly."

"I hate you."

If she had a point, I couldn't see it past the pulsating mob of American flags in our future. Not to mention the fact that James didn't have a gay bone in his entire body. Gay jeans, gay cardigans, and maybe even a slight case of gay face, fine. His bones, however, were anything but—trust. But at my twenty-seventh birthday party, he spent no less than an hour chatting up the two fiercest guys there, my gay husbands Antonio and Ricky. Most recently, Ricky had spent a small fortune at the Co-op in Georgetown just to get a closer look at James, who worked the register in between law school classes. I considered him safe until Antonio tapped me on my shoulder.

"Who *is* that?" he asked, doing a bad job of hiding a finger pointed in James's direction behind his upturned palm.

"Who? James?" I was buzzed.

"Yeaaaaaah . . . is he gay?" he asked, whispering in my ear as if the answer was already understood.

"Um, no, honey. He's mine." We slept together for the first time that night because (1) I needed birthday buns, and (2) I needed proof.

Somehow, Gina still got a "told you so" out of this. "And there you go," she said the next morning. Antonio's suspicion proved everything, and my sluttiness, nothing. What mattered was that James fit the profile, a constantly updated but well-edited list of identifying characteristics that made up the G.H.E.I. file, which started years before with a guy we'll call Winston.

Tall and good-looking with an island lilt only detectable when he answered the phone after six—"Good night?" That always threw me off. Another thing sticking with me was the time we went to see *Debbie Does Dallas: The Musical.* Not the musical part; that was my idea. Taye Diggs was sitting in the row directly in front of us. *Fine, no big deal, loved you in* Malibu's Most Wanted. But then afterward, as the porno-theater-goers crowded the sidewalk outside, Winston made a big show of patting his pants pockets. He claimed to have left something inside. Taye Diggs was still inside. I don't know if it was the way he'd whispered, "Hey, isn't that Taye Diggs?" or the overcompensating "Who gives a shit" way he acted when I answered, "Yes," but something in my spirit gave me the sneaking suspicion that Winston wanted to go in to take a closer look at Taye Taye. Maybe even sniff some of the air where he had stood or touch the seat where he had sat. I don't know; it was just a hunch. One that Gina was too thrilled to jump on. "I mean, dude, he did have on those Mexican Nikes." That's what she calls Nike Cortez Basics, which, in her jumbled opinion, are a very gay sneaker.

Aside from the Taye Diggs incident, there was also the issue of Winston's favorite position, which involved me lying face-down with my legs squeezed together and his on the outside.

"Like is he simulating a butt? Rear entry, I mean."

"Dude, I know what you mean, and, umm, yes."

So when a few months later, Winston told me that he was "uncomfortable being intimate" with me, instead of cursing him out, I considered myself lucky. Seeing as how I'd just been saved from a life of boredom being some hot guy's beard, I thought, Good riddance.

But not to the end of my gay phase. Next there was Jean Claude, whose real name was Frank. I noticed him courtside at a Nets game while I was shaking my pom-poms during TV time-outs. Yes, I used to be a professional cheerleader, a personal fact that has awarded me more ass than a lost puppy or a bigger bra size. Anyway, Jean Claude/Frank's lips were like something out of a racist comic book, and what he did with them was superhe-roic. But I couldn't get past how they looked attached to his face—always slightly parted, glistening with a "natural" gloss. So after a few weeks of struggling to explain his lips ("Dude, what's he supposed to do, cut 'em off?"), I took my own advice. Jean Claude/Frank asked me to "go with" him, and I laughed it off. He left offended.

Taylor's challenges were also physiological. Bored of going to the movies alone, I was on the lookout when I spotted a giant with a pointy bald head across a rooftop on a damp night out. Ignoring the likelihood of snow blindness, I stared directly into it as if it were a crystal ball, and like magic he turned around, his light browns bulging right back at me. Adrienne was concerned— "Does he have a hyperthyroid issue?"—and I was encouraged. I skied across the crowded rooftop and said, "You think I'm cute." Taylor called the next day, and casual dating ensued. High off that new-boy smell, I overlooked the fact that he said "put up" instead of "put away" and wore dress shoes with pressed denim. The squealing, though, was too high-pitched to ignore. "Play with my nipples," he'd moaned, out of breath on our first conjugal visit. *Um, okay, I guess, why not?*

My fingers had barely grazed them when it happened. There is no onomatopoeia in existence capable of sufficiently describ-ing the wild banshee mountain lion siren sounds that followed. I immediately snatched my hands back for fear of killing this man with kinkiness. His head shot up from the throes of passion, "Why'd you stop?" *Um, okay, I guess, why not?* More ungodly sounds. I was busy deejaying his pecs when he decided to high-kick things up a notch—literally lifting his lanky man gams up to his head, waiting for me to . . . do something. I was so impressed I forgot to throw up.

"I don't believe you." This was beyond even Gina's realm of comprehension.

"Swear to Zeus and CC Allah."

"So, what'd you do, dude?"

"Umm, pretended not to notice and went to sleep scarred but satisfied."

"You know you have AIDS now, right?"

"I hate you."

Was I ignoring the obvious or just obviously desperate? Or was it that I was looking for an excuse? A sheet of paper I could give my mother that read, "Listen, it's not her fault you don't have grandkids, blame it on *the gays,* signed Dr. What's-His-Guts." If dude was gay, well then obviously it wasn't going to work out. It wasn't my fault or anything. I mean it's not like the G.H.E.I. file was scaffolding meant to shore up all my issues with men or something. What I'm saying is that I was never the problem. Even I could admit to that, whether or not famous people could.

◇◇◇◇◇◇

"Star Jones finally filed for divorce," Gina said over IM one day.

"I saw that, tombout she made a mistake or whatnot by bringing the media into her life. Girl, stop. You made a mistake by marrying a gay man."

"Right. That'll do it. But, dude, that's what happens when you're forty and need a wedding . . . bad."

"What?" Gina gets paranoid sometimes, and the best thing to do is wait.

"That's why after I turn thirty-five, I'm all for having a wedding with no groom."

"For what purpose?"

"To get the fantasy out."

"That's just a 'happy to be single' party. We can do that right now. Or not."

"No, it has to have all the trimmings of a wedding, because seriously, how many of these weddings are about anything else but the woman anyway?" This from the same woman who once quoted Edith Ewing Bouvier Beale in a Gchat status message— "If you can't get a man to propose to you, you might as well be dead."

"But you need the man next to you," was my point. "He's an invaluable accessory." This was my attempt at injecting romance into our scenario.

"So hire one," Gina said. "That's probably just as likely to work out as your actual boyfriend, especially if your boyfriend is the gays."

We were enjoying this. Making our lives sound like an especially scary episode of *Law and Order SVU* or *New York Undercover*, if you want to get old-school. The musical montage at the beginning tells you everything you need to know, and the rest of the show is just filler for product placement. See, there's the master's in sociology strategically placed near her mid–twenties, and oh, look, there's the new condo in Leimert Park right in front of her thirties, and over there is the annual girls' weekend in Negril, Montego Bay, or somewhere in Mexico. Things had been set into motion since the first note of the theme song (elevator music?).

All we had to do was figure out how the pretty brunette ended up dead and alone in her apartment for four days with "Bohemian Rhapsody" blasting on repeat, her dog humping her broken heart and no one noticing.

There was one snag in the plot, though—none of these guys were, in fact, gay. Gay-ish? Maybe. But ready for a ride on the party bus down to Tangy Town—not so much. Once I traumatized Dexter, who Gina had warned me about after seeing him appear online in a fierce face (c) *Zoolander*. I told him one day I wished he was gay, because then we could be the black Will and Grace. "Then we could be together forever, no problem!" He said there was just one hitch—the doing the nasty with other dudes part. See? Not gay. Still, we carried on our detective work with associates from Carmen San Diego Community College, memorizing their down-low dossiers for midterms that would never come. *Marry you? Please. I know the truth, rootytooty69!* James–Taylor–Jean-Claude/Frank–Winston could have been any unsuspecting gentleman willing to bet on my personality while I picked apart his sexuality. My real job was to beat him to the punch before *I* got outed as an asshole.

Admitting my own perversion—namely egocentrality—was out of the question. Blaming it on the downpour of down-low hysteria was much easier. Especially since I've got this other friend—let's call her Stella—whose "boyfriend" really is gay. For real.

"She's so not familiar with his gayness," I told Gina on my way back from meeting Stella and her new manfy for brunch. Exhibit A, if you will.

"Why, what happened? What he do?" Whatever she was doing, she stopped to get the juice on the latest fruit.

"First off, he had on flip-flops. Then he ordered a cup of tea and drank it with a superflexed pinkie."

"Was it flexed, dude?"

"No, dude—superflexed."

I wanted to tell Stella that Eric, the black Canadian she claimed to be in love with, was super gay. Like totally, unquestionably gay. Like "I pair sandals I bought from Armani Exchange with smedium polo shirts" gay. More than a vibe, I got a vision from something bigger than us—a burning bush, let's say—and it was compelling me to tell Stella to stop, drop, and roll before Eric's flames got too intense. Despite the fact that she was an Easter Sunday Catholic, I knew she wouldn't believe me. Who would, besides Gi? Better to keep my mouth shut and my eyes open.

"Really? I didn't think Eric was all that gay when I met him." Adrienne was next on the phone tree.

"I don't even know why I'm telling you this." I sighed, annoyed by how totally in the dark she was. "Everybody knows your gaydar is all out of whack."

"Shut your face!"

"Right." It'd been a touchy subject—Adrienne's lack of a homosexual sense—since the Calvin situation. Picture freshman year, a handsome sophomore with hazel contacts, and a fresh-faced co-ed that went by the nickname "little big booty girl." They dated for just a few months, but in Columbia time, that was long enough to forever brand her as "Oh, who used to date Calvin?" And when he switched from mechanical engineering to modern dance, it became "Ha, who used to date Calvin!" Long after we were formally introduced to his "friend" from the Dance Theatre of Harlem, he'd still leave Adrienne messages on Facebook about how she'd gotten better with age, "like a fine wine." All that coupled with a protracted "pretty boy" phase had chipped Adrienne's credibility down to negative gazillion when it came to deciding who was down-low or just too slow.

Anyway. Stella.

She called me in the middle of the day and in tears because of some books she'd found of Eric's. He likes settling down with a good murder mystery? Not sooo gay. No, she said. These books were on something called "sarging." They'd just moved in together, and Stella was going through discarded boxes, not looking for evidence of his sexuality, mind you, just for the kitchen stuff. We immediately consulted Google. Sarge (verb): to go out for the explicit purpose of either: (1) working on skills to attract the opposite sex; or (2) putting those skills to effect. "Well, that could mean a lot of things," I said, hoping to sound confident while mentally placing this bit of hard evidence in Eric's G.H.E.I. file (*the lad doth overcompensate too much, methinks*). Stella thought he might be cheating. "With who?" I asked in a gentle child predator's voice, not wanting to sound too menacing as I primed her for my next line: "A man?"

She said something about a girl from work before I got the chance.

It was probably better that way, since we'd had trust issues in the past. Stella and I met at the 1998–99 CU cheerleading tryouts. I liked her long, curly hair and told her so. "Thanks, yours are cute too," she said, already fingering the *Poetic Justice*-style braids I was wearing then. Stella was from the valley, an auxiliary member of the Chicano Caucus, who for reasons that are still unknown almost exclusively dated black guys—correction, idiotic black guys. I was a virgin then, and she was . . . not. Once we were dating these two guys on the football team, roommates, and were listening to rap music in their dorm room when someone decided to cut the lights off. I left in a huff and heard about how funny it all was the next day from Stella. Right, hilarious.

Another time she called me at two in the damn morning crying about this midget with an African name who ran track. According to all the black girls on campus, he had a thing for white girls, and Stella was close enough. This was the same guy who told Stella that I'd called *her* a "white girl" behind her back. What I said was, "Why is it that you only date white girls?" Anyway, he dumped her for a Persian chick who looked just like her, and she was upset about it. "Crying over some retard is not okay," I was saying while some cabdriver yelled at her from the curb. "I-heehuh-did-heehuh-'nt-heehuh-have-heehuh-any-heehuh-money-heehuh." Of course, he'd broken up with her in the middle of the night, after doing it, in Harlem, and she'd made a dramatic, if penniless, exit back to Morningside Heights—a $6 ride. I told her to go upstairs to bed. The cabbie would get tired eventually.

We'd gotten over "white girl"–gate, but I always had the feeling that she had the feeling that I was secretly hating from the sideline—you know, since she was stealing all of our amazing black men. So I knew to keep certain opinions—the gay ones—to myself, even if the black guys Stella dated were fucking idiots. Take Herb, who firstly is named Herb, and who secondly was hideous, and thirdly lived in Jersey, and fourthly cheated on her with some fat girl. Stella had gone to his apartment—in fucking Jersey—unannounced one day and seen "fat white feet" from under the door. She left without knocking. I wasn't hating on her; I was trying to help.

Now there's Eric. I got this e-mail from her about a week ago: "So anyway, we've been going along nicely. Yesterday morning, we planned a date night for the evening. I took off to the library to work. Okay, now hold on to your seat, you are not going to believe this: Around 3:30 p.m., I got a call from him, but for some reason I didn't answer. I didn't feel like talking to him. So, I check the message immediately, and this is what he says: 'Hi Stella, it's Eric. Ummm . . . so I'm going to Amsterdam. I'll be back on July 4th around 5 p.m. I'll leave you my credit card in case you need anything.' Ten minutes later he called again, this time ON HIS WAY TO THE AIRPORT."

Apparently, his "acting class" had scored a "last-minute deal" to take a "sightseeing trip" to the red-light district of the world. Needless to say, Stella wasn't happy about this—Eric's thespian pursuits or his unknown proclivities. My tongue was losing muscle function from all the biting.

"He's out there sticking his penis in someone's butthole, dude." Gina was the only one I told. Promise.

"What is he doing, dude?!"

I told Stella that there was a slight, minuscule, almost-not-even-worth-talking-about chance that this guy was leading a "secret life." And finally she agreed—sort of.

"The fact that I'm not even sad right now means that this is long overdue," she wrote back. "If anything, I feel bitter because of the time I wasted. Eric must have always known that he could never truly give me what I need. I resent him a little for pretending to be that person."

Was he pretending, or was Stella? Because this wasn't the first glimpse she'd had of his "acting" skills. It was the weekend of her graduation from law school, and a spot on their pullout had been reserved in my name, and despite a slight hesitation about the proximity to which that would place me to the sounds of their lovemaking, I hopped on the Chinatown. No worries though, if there was any hanky-panky going on in there, I didn't hear. I did, however, get an earful from Stella immediately upon my arrival. The week before, she accidentally discovered through some very thorough cybersleuthing (they grow up so fast!) that he'd planned a trip to Vegas with his "boys" to "watch" the "ultimate fighting championship." On the day he was supposed to leave, he still hadn't said anything about it. While Eric was

out getting "coffee," Stella came and sat on my sofa bed to discuss her options—go blind or go ape-shit.

"Maybe he isn't going," I said, not even convincing myself.

"Maaaybe. . . ." she said, probably thinking up all the things
that are legal in Sin City.

She was cut off by the sound of the door unlocking. And
there was Eric, without a latte and with a lined-up fade. My
main concern was the permanent retinal damage I was risking
by zipping my eyes back and forth between the two of them like
a cornered wild thing.

They walked silently into the bedroom. Five minutes later,
Stella came out alone.

"He's going to Vegas."

"Whaaaaa?"

"He said that he didn't even really want to go, and that he'd
totally stay if I wanted him to, but the point is I want him to go.
I don't want him to feel like he can't be with his friends or whatever. I just wanted him to tell me."

It took him ten more minutes to pack a bag, and then he was
off to watch grown men manhandle each other in a giant steel
cage. Jesus, Stella. And now less than a month later, he was off
to Amsterdam with his "acting class."

"Dude, are they 'acting' gay?" Gina wanted to know.

Who *was* acting here—us or them? Because eventually Eric
came home, and instead of marching him down to the free clinic,
Stella took his ass back—literally. He'd sent her a bunch of e-mails
about her "beauty being the guiding light to his inner peace," and
they fell right back into the whole "we really love each other deep
down and it's been almost like two years, and we're professionals
so we might as well make something work even though we spend
most of our free time complaining about how much the other one
fucking sucks" thing. But instead of judging her, I recognized her.

If Gina was the gay monkey on my back, then I was riding Stella's. "Maybe Amsterdam is the community theater capital of the world," I told Gina, hoping that maybe I'd be right about something for once.

A few weeks later Stella and Eric were over (for good this time, maybe), and I walked into work after a high-profile date the night before that left me . . . unenthused. Emily, my white work wife, wanted to know all about it—is he really tall, does he really carry the president's nuts, does he have a gun or something, how do you feel about the term "power couple"?

"Eh, he's probably gay. He had on basketball shoes and weird socks . . . gay socks."

"Jesus, you think *every*body is gay."

"That's 'cause everybody *is* gay."

THE NEW B WORD

Sometimes it's hard to tell.

I've got this good friend who happens also to be black. He was in an important meeting for work when someone said, "nuclear's the new N word." Ahh, okay. That's fine. Just hold on a second while the rest of us dust off our universal translators. [Insert futuristic computing sounds here.] Got it. So, what you *meant* to say was that nuclear is the twenty-first century's version of something so vile it cannot be named—sort of like the Lord Voldemort of physics. What you did not mean to say was that nuclear energy is some nigger-shit.

Even with the aid of advanced Federation technology, the safe-for-work reaction to such highly paid stupidity is purely a game-time decision. Leap over the conference table to choke someone out *or* nod your head knowingly, all the while ignoring the piercing holes being drilled into your face by all the other cowards at the table.

Celebrations should be in order for all those nonpostal heroes who choose the latter. This same friend of mine sent out an e-mail asking whether or not he should feel some kind of way about the whole thing. I responded something like, "Well, I don't think he meant any harm by it." What *I* meant was, pretending your coworkers are philosophers as opposed to racists is most certainly the more spineless option. It's also a recession. So there you go.

The same principle applied to another e-mail I got.

"Maureen wants you to go out with Barack's body guy, Reggie Love. When can you do drinks?" It should be noted here that Maureen Dowd does not speak about herself in the third person, nor does she send her own e-mails. This was from Ashley, her assistant. When I first started at the *Times* two years before, Maureen was between assistants. The girl I replaced at the news desk applied for the job but didn't get it. Word around the fax machines was that she lacked a certain cool, which left Maureen with no one to show her how to do stuff. The calls would start coming in at around 11:00 p.m.

"Remember that character from Li'l Abner? Who always had the cloud over his head? What was his name?"

"Maureen?"

"I need to send the column up to New York. How do I do that?"

"You mean via e-mail?"

"Sure, yeah."

"Okay, first open up your Outlook by double clicking your mouse on the desktop icon, then go to 'compose mail,' which should be—"

"How 'bout you just come back here."

When Ashley, having met the cool specifications, arrived a week later, I looked upon her with pity and a bit of jealousy.

She'd be an all-things-normal oracle on columnists' row. I told her to start looking for her next job by year two, lest she get sucked into that black hole never to come out.

Then when I got my job at *Politico*, Maureen (Ashley) sent me flowers and a Mylar balloon that read "Congratulations" in crazy crayon letters. Once it was deflated, I stuck it above my computer with a pushpin. Passersby would nod in its direction, "From who?" and I'd answer "Maureen" without swiveling my chair around, leaving whomever to guess. "Maureen Dooowd, she means," chimed in my work wife Emily. "Oooh," they'd say.

After I'd spent a year covering Congressman What's-His-Guts' hair plugs and profiling his chief-of-staff's allergic reaction to jeans, the higher-ups asked if I wanted another shot at Barack Obama, since my South Carolina story was pretty decent. I was on my way back to Washington from Los Angeles, where I'd spent the weekend celebrating Gina's great-grandmother's one-hundredth birthday at the Chester Washington Golf Course of Gardena and trying to get over the fact that my sorority sister died at twenty-seven just the week before. For the sit-down-dinner portion of the afternoon, we got to choose between chicken, beef, or fish. When I answered "beef," a teenager in black pants gave me a piece of red construction paper. I figured it'd be a while and headed for the door before someone cued up the tape for a cousin's gospel rendition of "I Believe I Can Fly."

While I was outside admiring the neat carpet lines of the golf green, an old "boyfriend," probably bored on a Sunday, called to check in. I routinely reply to all just-being-polite personal inquiries the same way: "Good good." But I was worn down from a morning spent arranging "gold not yellow" roses with baby's breath while trying to keep the knot in my throat at bay. "Actually, life fucking sucks right now," I told him.

"Really? What's wrong? What happened?"

I entertained no thoughts of this man being able to compre-
hend, much less solve, any of my problems but wanted him to know
about them anyway. "Well, you remember my friend Adaoha? You
met her at that club that one time."

"Yeah, sure."

"Well, she died Thursday and I can't be alone in that fucking
rat-infested basement, so I'm in Cali for less than forty-eight
hours for this family thing with Gi. My life is a shambles."

"Jesus."

Calling on the Lord was the one thing I hadn't tried, and
unfortunately there was no time. "Wait, hold on. Actually, this is
work calling. I'll talk to you when I get back." He was probably
more relieved than I was; spilling your guts sounds pointless,
because it is. On the other line was the office, collectively wondering if I'd like to cover Obama's "race speech" in Philadelphia
on Tuesday. It was Sunday. Well, yeah, sure. Sounds great, but
did they know what was going on with me? By the way, sorry
about your friend. So can you do it?

Inside, my well-done brisket was waiting.

I spent the next three days perpetually exhausted. My flight
was delayed for no less than ten hours because of a computer
glitch, and the new citizen manning the SuperShuttle heard my
address in a different language, stealing even more hours from
me. The one night I spent in the bat cave was especially sleep-
less. A rat had set up shop under my bed, getting to work by
devouring the crotches of two pairs of Calvin Kleins and, if I was
ever able to dream, my eyeballs. Leaving every light on helped.
Plus, after too many weekends of rain my one closet was full of
mold. The shoes I planned for Philadelphia had been ruined in a
lovely shade of green—the kind of color that looks sophisticated
and old-worldly on once-bronzed generals riding horseback. I
took a wet towel to their soles and hoped no one would notice.

I rode in on the Amtrak "quiet car," figuring the likelihood of business commuter chitchat would be greatly reduced. So when my phone rang, I had to take it in the bathroom. Over the choo-chooing of the train and swish-swishing of the toilet bowl water, I could hear my boss asking what I thought the day would be like. I managed to say "historic" without choking.

Once inside the scrum of reporters, I found myself longing for the wide-open spaces of an Amtrak restroom. It was too late to pretend like I'd never made it, like I'd accidentally crapped my pants and fallen onto the third rail. Since that hadn't happened yet, I put on my "I so know what the fuck I'm doing" face and handed over my ID card when pressed. People seemed equal parts impressed and surprised when matching the name to my face, which made little to no sense because there was a carica-ture of me on our home page. A snarky blog once wrote, "Why is one of *Politico*'s only black writers Helena Andrews portrayed as a drinker? All of the other caricatures on their pages are pretty *vanilla*, if you catch our drift." I thought I looked cute comicized.

I was getting quotes from a Baptist preacher-minister-reverend-doctor when I spotted Maureen looking bored over by a group of reporters who'd converted their mics into light sabers, fighting to get to a man in rabbinical garb. I thanked Rev. Whatever-the-Hell and walked over to say hello, careful to avoid the cluster-fuck to my left.

"Maureen? Hey!" It took her a few minutes to register my existence, but once that was out of the way, an immediate flash of purpose lit up her face.

"I've got a guy for you. He's so hot, it's perfect." When I balked, she brought in reinforcements.

"Zeleny, Zeleny! Don't you think Reggie would be great for Helena?" She was surveying other page-one journalists from the campaign trail.

"Yeaaaaah." This reporter eyed me up and down with a finger at his temple—the international hand sign for "Give me a minute to think about it." "Yeaaaah, I could see that, I guess. Reggie Love, right?" I wasn't sure if his lack of enthusiasm was meant for me or Reggie. Either way, I was worried. And Reggie Love? Did this guy moonlight as a political porn star?

"I don't know, Maureen," I said, half protesting.

"Please. Don't be stupid. Ashley'll set it up." And then she disappeared inside the auditorium where Obama had just spoken about his awesome blackness, leaving me to wait to grab a few quotes from the rabbi.

Weeks went by, and I forgot all about loving Reggie, hoping Maureen had too, since white-people hot is never the same. I tried explaining this to Emily. "What about that guy on *The West Wing*?" she asked. I'm shaking my head no before she can finish. "You're crazy," she said. "He's hot." Impaired judgment aside, the idea of going out with a presidential candidate's bodyguard did sound sexy as hell. "Oh, what does your boyfriend do?" strangers would ask over highballs at Arianna Huffington's house. "Sacrifices his body for democracy on a daily basis. Yours?"

But I had my doubts after getting the e-mail: "Maureen wants you to go out with Barack's body guy . . ."

Ooooh, body *guy*, not *guard*. The fuck? Fantasy crushed. Expectations flattened as per the usual. What does that job title even entail? Maureen Dowd. Barack Obama! Reggie Love? This was my internal discourse.

Then Ashley BCC'd me on the one she sent to Reggie: "So, Maureen wants me to introduce you to our friend Helena Andrews. Are you free for a drink tomorrow night in D.C.?"

Our friend? Tee-hee-hee. Okay, fine, I'll go. But only as a personal favor to my Pulitzer Prize–winning pal.

The three of us decided to meet at a bar/lounge/restaurant called Marvin over by my house. The place is cool because everyone says so, and since the lights are never turned on all the way, nobody could tell one way or the other. The manager is this black guy with high-water pants, Malcolm X glasses, and a fro-hawk. Ashley and I (I needed both moral support and a possible cover) ate dinner while we waited . . . and waited, and waited.

After two hours and as many e-mails, Reggie finally showed up wearing his workout clothes—gym shorts, an "Obama for Change" T-shirt, and tube socks. I was in tight jeans and three-inch heels, wishing I'd stayed home. I got an "I do it to white girls" vibe from him. In person he explained that he'd just had his first day off in months, which in and of itself speaks volumes for his work ethic and maybe his ability to commit. Check. Then he kept talking. Turns out he'd gotten so drunk with his buds back home that'd he'd passed out and missed his flight to Washington. If he got any points for being honest, they were immediately negated by his adolescence. I was missing *Sex and the City* reruns for this.

Reggie was cute in a way-too-tall way. The chair he sat in didn't have a chance. Reminded me of one of those scenes where parents are forced to sit in their second-grader's desk for Back to School night. This thing might turn out just as clumsy. His head was too pointy, purposefully shaved in a way that inadvertently highlighted the isosceles shape. I thought about the crazy Gigantor babies we'd have and decided to do the planet a favor by not liking this guy. He had a boyish smile that would have suckered me in if not for the basketball shorts. Like, thanks for stopping by on your way to Bally's, guy.

The three of us made klutzy conversationalists for an excruciating hour. "So you work for *Politico*?" "Yeah." "Well, this is all off the record!" "Right." I was playing it too classy and casual to ask about his famous boss and instead imagined the two of them sitting in a sauna after a hard game, towels wrapped around their waists ever so loosely. He said he was rarely in Washington, which I took as a preemptive strike right in line with the Bush Doctrine.

But then I was confused, because just a few moments later, he slapped my left butt cheek kind of hard with an open palm. Google said he was a college basketball player, so I wanted to get his thoughts on the pervasive homoeroticism displayed in men's sports because that's what I do—I'm a ballbuster. Better than explaining it to me using his words, Reggie decided to demonstrate the innocence of the ass pat by going all medieval on mine. His hands were quite large, though . . . so make that strike two and a half.

With a searing backside, I excused myself to the bathroom—which was quickly becoming one of my favorite places to unwind—to call Gina to discuss my options. I mentioned the word *square* multiple times.

"Dude, how the hell you gonna call somebody else a square? And what options do you have right now?" If she was right, I was well on my way to doing exactly what Dex told me not to—dropping Perfect Guy for a not-so-perfect one.

When I got back to our table, Ashley had already left (smooth), and Reggie offered to escort me home.

He walked on the outside of me like a true gentleman—an adjective I'd never used to describe a "date" before—and said he'd be "honored" if I'd go out with him again the next time he was in town. Standing outside my door, I said yes for the same reasons he'd asked—out of duty and nostalgia. When I stood on my tippy toes, we were able to hug, both knowing this hours-long detour was finally over with. Back to the campaign for him and complaining for me.

"I think she thought that you were two people at the top of your game and that you guys would click," explained Ashley the next day, adding that according to some people "Reggie was like the coolest person on the trail."

"And you're sure it wasn't more like, 'Hey, here's two young black people I know, so why not let's get them together,' Ash?"

"No, no, no, no, no."

A profile on Reggie came out in the *Times* a week later. In it, Barack said, "There's no doubt that Reggie is cooler than I am. I am living vicariously through Reggie." I developed major reservations concerning the future president's hipness acumen but looked up my voter registration info anyway. Then *People* magazine voted Reggie one of the top twenty-five hottest bachelors of the year, and I had a mini-breakdown.

"Dude, did you see the *Times* story and this thing in *People*? This fucking guy is everywhere."

"I'm looking now," said Gina. "Yeah. Gay."

"Dex called it an ode to bromance," I told her, and yes, I'd told Dexter all about my date and he was kind enough to act jealous, going on and on about how Reggie holds Barack Obama's nuts in a briefcase for a living. Actually, they were MET-Rx chocolate roasted-peanut protein bars, but what did that matter?

Really, I was the one going crazy, finding fault in a nationally ranked bachelor in favor of a retard who made nonsensical gonad jokes and couldn't tell the difference between friend feelings and more-than-friend feelings. I wished I could get Lisa Nowak on the horn. Honk if you have impossibly high expectations that never get met so you'll settle for an idiot with a law degree and commitment issues. Sure, Reggie was no Cliff, but perhaps he was something even better. But then again, white people hot is never the same.

"You're so crazy pants. He's super friggin' hot. Look at him in this magazine," said Emily, doing the ta-dah hands in front of her computer, which was displaying a full-screen photo of one Reggie Love in the kind of oversize business suit pro athletes wear.

"Why do white people always think black men who take baths are the hottest things since Morgan Freeman?" I asked. "That guy is in his seventies, you know."

"You're the whitest black girl I know!"

Now how to take this? Sometimes I wanted to go through my entire life story as a way of explanation: "Well, my mom has a high-falutin' accent—basically she speaks the King's English, I spent a lot of my childhood on an island with no black people, I went to an Ivy League college. So don't let the white girl accent fool you—I was raised in da 'hood. Compton, Cali-forn-yah to be exact, pimpin'. Left Co-ast!" By now I've thrown some C's on it, having just finished up the complicated heel-toe known to a certain demographic as "the Crip walk."

"You're not from the ghetto. You went to Columbia. Please." Emily always felt it acceptable—nay, necessary—to knock my street creds. Almost as often as I felt the need to offer them up. One time I invited her and her now-husband, then-fiancé, to the fish fry I have at my house every year.

"You eat fried fish?!"

"Emily, I'm black." That's as far as I got. Because, really, she was a good friend of mine. A friend I allowed to ask me mildly racist questions because, really, who the hell else is going to answer them for her? A friend for whom I'd Googled, printed, and pushpinned the lyrics to "Ebony and Ivory." A friend who once asked me if it was "ghetto" around where I lived, and to whom I'd given an unflinching "yes." We were walking down U

Street—like 125th in Harlem, but with many more "hot spots" and many fewer black Jesus posters—when she said she had something for me to see. Get ready, Emily said, for "the most ridiculous thing" ever in "five, four, three, two . . ." It was the McDonald's walk-up window.

"Isn't that the most hilarious thing ever?"

"Umm, they have that so crackheads don't shank some poor guy on the midnight shift for a McFlurry."

"I know, but still!" She had the innocent wide eyes of someone who'd never bit into a delicious McRib sandwich. I bet they never even sold them in Indiana. Sad. If I took her under my wing, then maybe she wouldn't get henpecked (shanked) by a real black person sometime in the immediate future.

The most egregious indictment of my racial invisibility happened, coincidentally enough, on my way to Emily's wedding the next summer. I'd planned the trip with another girl named Emily because we were both taking the cheap flight into Kentucky and then "driving" the hour and a half to Evansville, Indiana. I put "driving" in quotes because, as previously stated, I do not now nor do I ever plan on obtaining an actual license to operate a motorized vehicle of any kind, but no one says "I'm gonna *ride* from point A to point B," because it sounds too passive-aggressive. Basically, I needed a chauffeur, and for half the rental car costs, this chick was up for the task.

Chauffeur Emily and I had suffered through work wife Emily's day-long bachelorette party and the string of mass e-mails leading up to it. The only one I added to the thread was about cup and panty size: a subject no one else would touch. Chauffeur Emily sent me an e-mail saying, "Thank God," and we immediately got to synchronizing our flight schedules.

The Raleigh-Durham International Airport is ghetto—period. There are no good places to eat, and the seats smell like missed connections mixed with dreams deferred. We had an hour lay-over and were forced into Maui Tacos. Between bites of burrito, the two of us waxed poetic about overblown Washington men and my coincidental singledom.

The guys in town, we agreed, had inflated stomachs and egos to match. I was supposed to have a date for the wedding—James, the one who announced at a pizza place that being an intern twenty floors up from my cubicle precluded the possibility of us getting "romantically involved." This from the guy who con-vinced me to swallow his man juice because anything else was "emasculating." So the District, we decided, just wasn't the place to meet anybody normal—although she and her lawyer were currently redoing their kitchen. Plus, everybody's gay! And then there's the shitty club situation! With like two places to go, you end up seeing the same people over and over and over again.

"I mean, everybody goes out to all the same crappy places," said Chauffeur Emily, picking through her beans and rice. Mouth full of pico de gallo, I nodded my agreement. "Plus, if you want to go to like a big club, especially on a Saturday, it's always all these minorities."

Wait, what? I looked around to make sure we were still in this zone and not the Twilight one. She was already folding a napkin around her leftover burrito, headed for the trash cans. Alone at the table, I wondered whether or not I'd heard her cor-rectly. Minorities? That's me, right? But I don't think she meant to include me in that category. Had we gotten so chummy in the security line that Emily had mistaken my bronze skin for a tan, a costume, a cover?

Adrienne was always wary of me "getting too cool" with "the whites," as Gina called them. "You can't trust them," is what she'd say when I'd tell her about a bitch session work wife Emily and I had over burgers at Ruby Tuesdays. "I know you think she's your friend and ish, but be careful. She's not your friend friend." Ah, the difference a double makes.

What was this, *West Side Story*? Or, even more apropos, the "Bad" video? I didn't straighten Chauffeur Emily out, because I didn't want our travel plans unraveled. Once again my lack of a driver's license was making the ride uncomfortable. Especially since I was in charge of Google Maps for the next two hours. How would the navigating have gone if instead of "Turn right here," I shouted, "Excuse me, I am black, and you, my good lady, are out of or-dah"? Or pointed out the street sign that read, AIN'T I A WOMAN? Nope, I was a Shark with no teeth.

So we got to Evansville no problem, and as long as I kept my mouth shut, the weekend would go off without a hitch. Because we were here to see my good friend get hitched, and bringing up racism at the rehearsal dinner is just plain rude. Later that night when I met Chauffeur Emily downstairs for a glass of "the red one" at the Evansville Airport Marriott's bar, she looked shocked. "How'd you get your hair like that? It's gorgeous." I wrapped my new ponytail around my wrist and whispered, "un-be-weave-able, isn't it?" She didn't get it, and I promised to show her later.

◇◇◇◇◇◇

"Dude, did you see that article about the blacks and best friends forever?" When Gina gets super hyped about an "article," I stop what I'm doing and click on the link.

"Please hold." It only took minutes to get enlightened. "Are you serious right now? This is awesomeness."

"Am I your BBF?" she asked.

"If not you, then who?"

It'd been a week since Emily's nuptials, and my spinelessness in the face of wedding favors. A reporter from the *Los Angeles*

Times had obviously been stalking me. In the article "Buddy System," the paper coined the acronym BBF, or the "black best friend." I was immediately reminded of the "LMBAO"—"laughing my black ass off"—phase we went through online in college, which in turn gave birth to my favorite Chicana's cyber acronym of choice, LMMAO.

Anyway, according to the *Times*, BBFs were a pop culture phenomenon in which black actresses were repeatedly cast as characters whose "principal function is to support the heroine, often with sass, attitude and a keen insight into relationships and life." They were most often "gorgeous, independent, loyal and successful. . . . And even though they are single or lack consistent solid relationships, BBFs are experts in the ways of the world, using that knowledge to comfort, warn or scold their BFF." (The latter being their "best friend forever," otherwise known as the white heroine.) I was pissed I didn't come up with this shit first. They were typing my pain with their fingers, writing my life with their words.

My BBF blues song was sung mostly at work. The *New York Times*, *Politico*, even *Oprah* magazine, were all "pretty vanilla." I remember complaining to a young black reporter whom I admired that the folks at the *Times* always seemed so afraid to ask me about my life after five. "It's not like I was beating African drums all weekend." Laughing, she said that sometimes it pays to be the only black girl in the room. "Everybody here knows who I am."

When I got tired of being asked about Michelle Obama, I started freelancing stories for TheRoot.com, and one of my bosses referred to the *Washington Post*–owned Web site as "some blog." I got the most hits on a piece about Jennifer Hudson's character in *Sex and the City: The Movie*, basically comparing her to a twenty-first-century Mammy: big-breasted with plenty of down-home love to offer her hapless white charge. The story got dozens of comments from women who were tired of being the "magical Negro." One chick said that *I* had low self-esteem, and another claimed I just wanted to be part of the in crowd. Duh. But the feedback from someone calling herself "Uppity Negress" got to me:

"I think because we are older, Generation X, we are set in our sub-demographics and with me not being married and with the same exact interests, I don't fit in or get invited. That has a lot to do with my being single and Black with a tongue that tends to pronounce that there are elephants in the room. That is not *SATC's* responsibility to work this out for me and my White Peers. It's upon us."

I guess my tongue, having been tied for so long, was suffering from atrophy. And if there were elephants in the room, stepping over their massive poop was always preferable to stepping in it. The thing is, Uppity Negress, as BBFs we're all too busy being defined by that negative space, by what we are *not*, to actually focus on what we are. We aren't weak. We aren't white. We aren't idiots. That leaves: strong, black, women. I wish I could say we were goddesses. But the BBF is anything but divine; in truth, she is destroying us.

Helena to Gina: "Dude, I am in these streets right now fighting for survival!"

"*What are you doing, dude?*"

"Fighting. For. My. Damn. Life. Do I need therapy?" I knew what her answer would be. Gina was a sociologist. "I was watching *Sex and the City* last night," I said. "That episode where Carrie sees a shrink."

"Everybody needs therapy, dude. Especially you. I'm totally familiar with how you get down."

I had been very down. Adaoha was gone. Adrienne and Stella were studying for the bar, and I hadn't spoken to them in weeks.

Kia was busy with three kids now. Evelyn was getting married. And Dex, the dum-dum, was in Indianapolis for the summer, learning about how not to be with me. But who cares about Dex? We broke up right before he left during a torturous car ride to work.

"So you don't want me to visit this summer?"

"No," he said. "I don't think you should. I mean, how would that help things?"

Things? Where are these things everyone keeps talking about? And how do I get rid of them?

I started ignoring my mother's calls and spent entire weekends in the farthest reaches of the bat cave, not caring that the rats had probably given me the bubonic plague. Rashes broke out on my arms that hadn't been visible since 2004, when West Point Willy told me he got some other chick pregnant. I was drinking a $4.99 bottle of Whole Foods wine on a good day, two on a bad one. The fainting spell behind me, I was still too scared to walk over the Key Bridge from Virginia to Georgetown because jumping seemed all too doable. I cried at the office twice and refused to look up from my computer screen when someone asked me a question. Emily gave me a sign that read, "Out to lunch: If not back by 5, out to dinner." I hated everyone, especially this jackass named Jonathan who insisted on saying, "Hello Hah-laaay-nuh," every time he walked past my desk. We'd shared an excruciating slow dance at Emily's wedding. She forwarded the picture evidence to all the cool kids, and I got mad because my face looked greasy.

In short, I was in a weird place. Every morning, Emily would tell people who stopped by our cubicle that I was "grumpy-pants today." So they kept walking past without saying "hello." Most days I appreciated the intervention, but on others I just wanted someone to fucking say "hello" to me! Someone other than Jonathan (and sometimes even him).

"He just wants to flirt with you but doesn't know how," she explained. "He's scared."

"Why the hell is everybody so scared of me around here? Is it because I'm black?"

"No," she said. "It's because you're a bitch."

YOUR SIXTEEN CENTS

I might be forced to have Frances committed way earlier than previously planned. The woman's got a crazy case of "grandbabies." In her room, nailed up on the wall opposite her bed, is a fucking baby christening dress, white, lacy, and with a satin bow in the middle. Its hem is a little dirty, most likely because she found it in a trash can or maybe stole it off an unsuspecting baby at a baptism—either way, it ain't mine and it ain't hers. I refuse to ask about it because the answer might make me an accomplice. A white baby prom gown that needs a good spot clean is tacked to a wall in my mother's bedroom like how a teenager puts up posters or prisoners a pinup. I just thought that needed repeating.

I'm not sure exactly when it happened—the metaphysical and temporal shift in my mother's mind when I went from being her prized only daughter to her only hope for progeniture. When the name Helena became synonymous with her dashed hopes.

It had to have been last fall, when I turned twenty-eight and spent a stimulus check on a purebred named Miles. Her first response was, "You girls nowadays would rather get a dog than a baby!" Significant because it was the first time I'd heard her say the word *baby* with such craving, such conviction—as if it were a prophecy being revealed to me in pieces she'd been hiding. The word was magic I just didn't know yet. Each side now revealed, we both laughed that nervous laugh, and I changed the subject to something more suitable for mothers and their adult-ish daughters—boys.

Jake, yea *that* Jake—the porno pizza deliveryman of my dreams—and I were "dating." Turns out the tension *was* sexual that night we sat on my sofa watching *Seinfeld* and typing on our laptops. He just really had a lot of work to do. And me, well, you know. I'm a work in progress. Anyway when I told her that formerly "just friends" Jake and I were something more than, she screamed. Like this undulating Amazonian mating call type scream.

"But he doesn't want to have kids anytime soon, woman," I said, ripping off her baby Band-Aid.

"How do you know?" she shot back. "Right now, of course not. But laaaater."

When I told Jake this, he laughed, remembering the time his own mother showed up at his house with a "lap protector" after watching something on the news about how much damage a laptop's heat can do to a man's spermies. Maybe things would work out between us, after all. Grandbaby-crazed mothers? Check. He'd found out from Google how much a temporary vasectomy would cost, and I considered the fee nominal.

A month later when I almost broke up with him because he works like a maniac, leaving him precious little time to be obsessed with me, Frances screamed again. This time *at* me. Said I was being selfish.

We were on opposing teams again, and I should've seen it coming. Around Christmastime, my mother's baby craving became impossible to ignore. My cousin's oldest son—the first kid I babysat for free—had just had his own son. Right. The baby was the first member of our family's sixth generation, and apparently the first baby ever. My mother cradled her great-great-nephew, looking down at him—and across the room at me, expectantly.

The next week, it all came out in the open. We were on our way to Gina's great-grandmother's house to eat gumbo for good luck in the New Year. Randomly, between radio commercials, Frances admitted that she could not, in all fairness, harass me about having a baby, since she was almost thirty years old when she decided to have me.

"Ma, you know I'll be twenty-nine in less than a year, right?" I asked, immediately regretting that decision.

"Oh," she paused. "Right."

Then, to either shock or silence her, I said it wouldn't be the end of the world if an alien life form decided not to invade my womb for nine months. It wouldn't do irreparable damage to my self-worth or anything. "Lots of women are childless, and somehow they find a way to go on," I said. We rode the rest of the way talking about everything but the ten-pound hypothetical baby in the backseat. I thought the issue was tabled until she announced, unsolicited, at Gina's great-grandmother's dining table that she'd never have her own grandchildren—ever.

"Do you know what Lena said in the car . . . ?" Gina and I thought it wise to hide in the kitchen.

If you've ever been to a wedding, funeral, or father-daughter purity ball, then you've sat—perhaps teary-eyed—through John

Mayer's "Daughters," basically the sound track of every Lifetime movie in existence. It's about how some girl got so messed up by her parents that now she can't truly love the man standing on her steps with his heart in his hand or whatever.

The last two lines of the hook are something like a eulogy: "Girls become lovers, who turn into mothers. So mothers, be good to your daughters, too." Why not "girls become lovers who turn into . . ." something other than mothers? First ladies, maybe. Whatever, I get that it's hard to rhyme and be politically correct, but since when did the act of becoming a mother become the last rite of passage between a mother and a daughter? As if handing down the ability to procreate is somehow confirmation of a mother's love, or perhaps a job well done.

Funny, Stella's definition of womanhood is also tied to work. Having broken up with Eric for real this time, she says she's good on "pushing a baby out of my body like a damn animal. I'm a professional." Adrienne thinks because she's a lawyer she has to have a baby "like two years ago," but admits she'd go bat shit if she were ever to actually be with child.

Gina just wants cash. Her dad, Carl, gave all the women who qualified $50 for Mother's Day last year. Much like her womb, Gina's card was empty.

"When I complained that he was incentivizing pregnancy, he gave me sixteen cents out of his pocket," she told me later. "I informed him that that was not on par and that I was going to get preggers just to rectify the situation. I mean, what the fuck?"

I wished I knew what Frances was thinking sometimes. Maybe then I'd know how to respond when she says something like, "Well you know you could always just adopt a baby from Africa like Madonna or that skinny girl, what's her name?"

"Angelina Jolie, Mommy"—even when being downgraded from a daughter to a diaphragm, I still want to help.

"Yep, that's the one."

My theory, when I really think about it, is that my mother—being a lesbian and hippie, and having never been on the "right" side of society's norms—probably just wants me settled, safe. She wants to make up for convincing me that Darin the lovable stalker wasn't a complete whack job or for not being there when I was on a cold clinic table not having a baby at nineteen. When I was a kid, Frances always introduced me the same way—as her "first and last." It made me proud. Made me feel important. Still does. So for right now, I like being a daughter—only.

And that size-12-months baby prom dress on her wall? The one she seriously said was for her "granddaughter," after I finally got the guts to ask about it? It still creeps me the fuck out. But then again, it gives me something close to hope.

Acknowledgments

This is the hard part. Or should I say the "most likely to get me into deep shit with whomever I fail to mention" part. So despite lacking the luxury of an Oscar podium to hide behind, I'm still going to go off the cuff and pretend like I didn't know this was about to happen.

First off, thanks to Gina, who in 1996 wrote in my yearbook, "You and you're [sic] men, or boyz [sic] or whatever they are. You need to stop jockin'!" Words to live by. And thanks to the other two women I'm totally gay for—Adrienne and Raquel. One for screaming, "finish the effin' book!" as a matter of routine, and the other for getting me drunk on a routine basis and therefore necessitating the demands of the former. Next item on my mental napkin is 1902 9th Street NW, the headquarters of my disillusioned adulthood. Thanks to the rats, the bums, and the heartbreakers thereabouts.

Without the Gail Ross Literary Agency—Howard, Gail, Anna—this book would still be in my head. Without my editor at Harper Collins, Jeanette Perez, some might wish it had stayed there. Also, I'd like to pour some out for the folks at Collins—Serena and Bruce—who after hearing my spiel said something along the lines of "you're the most awesome person ever," which despite being obvious helped a great deal. Big shout-out to Ryan Grim, who told me writing books was a "good side hustle." Liar. And Sherly Chun for calling me a Korean taxi for that one meeting I had (I'm a woman of my word).

Lastly, there is no synonym of thanks that is great enough to be applied to my mother, Frances Vernell Andrews. We knew each other before there was an us to know. I am a writer because she saw the fake Chinese hieroglyphics Sharpie penned on the dry-erase board and instead of having me committed bought me a journal. I am grateful. You are the greatest.